“Given how ancient and ubiquitous our human suffering is, one would think that we would have said all that can be said about it. But it is because of its very nature that we continually, deeply need voices that remind us afresh of what it means to suffer as we follow Jesus. With *When the Journey Hurts*, it is to this need that Kelly M. Kapic, M. Elizabeth Hall, and Jason McMartin have so compassionately written, while remaining unflinching in the face of how anguishing our suffering can be. Read this for clarity. Read this to find mercy. But most of all, read this to know that you are not alone on the road of suffering that you and others are traveling.”

Curt Thompson, psychiatrist and author of *The Deepest Place* and *The Soul of Desire*

“In times of suffering, we often seek advice from others who have gone through similar difficulties, hoping to find comfort, reassurance, and answers to our search for how we, too, might survive and thrive. Never satisfied with trite or predictable responses, the authors instead lay out a potential roadmap through the dark days of anguish, illness, and trouble with fresh words of hope that stirred my soul.”

Kay Warren, founder of Hope for Brighter Tomorrows and author of *Choose Joy: When Happiness Isn't Enough*

“*When the Journey Hurts* is a beautifully written and deeply moving book that invites readers to encounter God's presence in the midst of suffering. Kelly M. Kapic, M. Elizabeth Hall, and Jason McMartin bring rare wisdom, honesty, and compassion to some of life's hardest questions. Their words offer both comfort and courage, helping us see that faith can grow stronger and more tender in the face of adversity. This book is a true gift to the church and to anyone walking through difficult seasons.”

Jamie Aten, cofounder of Spiritual First Aid and Blanchard Chair of Humanitarian and Disaster Leadership at Wheaton College's Humanitarian Disaster Institute

“‘The journey through suffering, while unwanted, can be the road to flourishing—the hard road to glory.’ The authors back up that hope-filled statement with stirring testimonies, careful research, and penetrating insight that reveal the mysterious value of suffering. They don't celebrate or explain away our pain; instead, they remind us that God is with us in our trials and that they are never without purpose. After reading *When the Journey Hurts*, you'll be convinced that, even in life's fiercest storms, God is redeeming what once threatened to undo us.”

Vaneetha Rendall Risner, author of *Watching for the Morning*

"A question Dallas Willard often asked was, 'Does the gospel we preach and teach bring comfort and strength, hope and meaning, to those who are suffering? If it does not, it is not Jesus' good news.' This book brings the gospel to those who are suffering. It is the best book I have read on the subject of how to find purpose in and through suffering."

James Bryan Smith, author of *The Good and Beautiful God*

"*When the Journey Hurts* addresses two difficult, timeless questions: How can I make sense of my suffering? And how can I best deal with suffering? This book uniquely offers both biblical and psychological insights that can be immediately applied to your life or the lives of those you love. It is full of stories, insights, and hope for those who suffer. I hope you will prayerfully read it and also share what you have learned with a friend."

Sean McDowell, professor of apologetics at Talbot School of Theology, author, and YouTuber

FINDING MEANING IN SUFFERING
FOR HEART, MIND, AND SOUL

WHEN THE JOURNEY *hurts*

M. ELIZABETH LEWIS HALL,
KELLY M. KAPIC, AND JASON McMARTIN

An imprint of InterVarsity Press
Downers Grove, Illinois

InterVarsity Press
P.O. Box 1400 | Downers Grove, IL 60515-1426
ivpress.com | email@ivpress.com

InterVarsity Press® is the publishing division of InterVarsity Christian Fellowship/USA®. For more information, visit intervarsity.org.

Cover design: Faceout Studio
Interior design: Daniel van Loon
Cover images: © Daria Zaseda / DigitalVision Vectors via Getty Images

ISBN 978-1-5140-0849-2 (print) | ISBN 978-1-5140-0850-8 (digital)

Printed in the United States of America ♾

Library of Congress Cataloging-in-Publication Data
A catalog record for this book is available from the Library of Congress.

33 32 31 30 29 28 27 26 | 12 11 10 9 8 7 6 5 4 3 2 1

To my father, Philip Lewis,

who modeled how to walk through suffering

with grace and gratitude before Jesus took him home

shortly after this book was finished.

Liz Hall

To Tabitha Kapic,

my beautiful bride of thirty-two years, I thank God

for your ongoing courage and faith amid the long and

exhausting storm of pain that never seems to end,

yet you endure it with grace and faithfulness.

Kelly Kapic

To the Crawford family, in memory of Scott (1975-2020).

Jason McMartin

CONTENTS

PREFACE

SUFFERING

THE BAD NEWS AND THE GOOD NEWS

"At least now we know."

Six years of wondering. Six years of countless medical tests and doctors. Six years of waiting.

It started two years after being declared "cancer-free." Seemingly out of nowhere, Tabitha (Kelly's wife) weakened suddenly and began to experience harsh pain emanating from her wrists and ankles. That's how it started one day in May, and it's only gotten worse, moving through her limbs and deeper into her body. Never a day free from the grip of pain and physical weakness.

In those first years, we didn't know exactly what was causing it. Numerous doctor visits and tests failed to provide us with answers. But now, as we sat there at the Mayo Clinic, the healthcare team delivered an official diagnosis of the two underlying issues. We were grateful to receive information assuring us that these problems were real and we were not crazy. Unfortunately, we also learned that there was no current solution for either problem. No medication, no physical therapy, and no surgery could resolve the issues. Tabitha would likely face these realities for the rest of her life. Getting this news, I (Kelly) wondered how Tabitha might respond and what I should say.

I'll never forget the resilience and courage she showed when she spoke: "At least now we know. For years we have been trying to find a way around the storm, but now we know there is no other way. We have to sail through it."

Amid this deeply discouraging news, Tabitha's bravery and resolve gave us both a new perspective. We needed to stop imagining we could escape this hurricane, and instead we needed to start figuring out what it meant to navigate our journey through it.

None of us like pain, so we have become marvelously creative at finding ways to go around it. We ignore, minimize, and deny it. Or maybe we try to wall it off. We tell ourselves and others it isn't so bad. Rub some dirt on it. We insist it serves a greater purpose. But at the end of the day, the path takes us through suffering, not around. And suffering is part of everyone's journey, not just Tabitha's. It hits us all sooner or later, in big or small ways. No one is exempt. No one gets a pass on suffering. No one.

The Christian story tells us that this is not how life should be. Sin's entrance into the world twisted the human heart and distorted the world God had created as a place where we could flourish. Most importantly, sin threatened to keep us from the source of life, God. Painful suffering and tears resulted from sin's entrance into the world—what is sometimes called "the fall." We do recognize that the physical sensation of pain can be understood as a positive gift (for example, your skin senses the heat of a flame and therefore alerts you to remove your hand before you get hurt). But this kind of pain is different from the suffering related to the effects of the fall.[1]

The Christian tradition has long held that the introduction of sin into the world brought about all kinds of negative forms of suffering, affecting everything from our relationships to our bodies. This does not mean we can or should attribute our suffering to a specific sin we have committed. But it does mean that sin has generally worked its way into God's good creation, twisting and defiling and making suffering an inevitable part of our lives. Although Jesus' death and resurrection have dealt a death blow to sin and suffering, we will continue to experience their lingering effects in our relationships with God, others, creation, and ourselves until Jesus returns.

To add insult to injury, suffering rattles the foundational ways we understand our world. As if the basics of our suffering weren't enough—the grief associated with loss, the physical pain of illness, the anger at betrayal—we also feel the ground shift beneath our feet. Affliction can shatter our assumptions about ourselves, our world, and our place in the world.

Who am I if the loss of my child means I am no longer a mother?

What kind of world do I live in if a random virus can wipe out millions of people?

What is the purpose of my life if this injury means I can't pursue my career as an athlete?

Events don't make sense. The world as we know it disappears. Our very identity, our sense of who we are, may be challenged. Moving through suffering requires a process of rebuilding our sense of meaning.

But there is good news. Even though suffering causes pain, the way it damages our meaning system—our working assumptions about ourselves, our world, and our place in the world—creates an opportunity. God can redeem our suffering. Challenges to our meaning system allow us to build a better and stronger meaning system, which can lead to a fuller life. We can leave behind mistaken, distorted, or insufficient assumptions about the world. We can develop a clearer vision of what life is about, what is important, and who we are. In God's mercy, our suffering can even lead to our flourishing. In fact, the psychological research suggesting a connection between suffering and flourishing is so strong that it has led one prominent psychologist to refer to suffering as "the hard road to the good life."[2] Suffering can lead us more deeply into Jesus.

In Matthew 7, Jesus compared a person who built their house on a rock with someone who built it on sand. When the hard things in life came—the rains and winds and floods—the house on the sand came tumbling down. All our houses are a little vulnerable. We don't examine our foundations until cracks start showing up in the walls and ceilings. Suffering allows us to look carefully and see if our foundations are substantial enough to support us for the long haul. Have we built on sand or on rock? If our foundations are sandy, God, in his goodness, lovingly helps us rebuild.

We know a bit of this through experience. Liz Hall is a clinical psychologist and a professor at Rosemead School of Psychology, Biola University. She has been a therapist for almost thirty years and also teaches adult Sunday school regularly at the church she has attended since her college years. While her research has always been at the intersection of psychology and theology, she began investigating how Christians cope with suffering after her own experience with cancer. At age forty-five, while her two boys were in their early teenage years, she was diagnosed with stage two breast cancer and endured a year of multiple surgeries and invasive treatments, as well as ongoing health concerns caused by the chemotherapy.

Kelly Kapic has taught theology at Covenant College for twenty-five years. Not only has he listened to and walked alongside students and others as they've navigated suffering, but his own family has also traveled this difficult path. When their two children were both under six years old, Tabitha was diagnosed with cancer in 2008. As noted above, after going through her surgeries and treatments, she was eventually declared cancer-free, only to have severe chronic pain and fatigue develop in 2010—conditions that have not disappeared or lessened. Through these experiences, Kelly has been motivated to research and write on suffering, including his book *Embodied Hope: A Theological Meditation on Pain and Suffering*.[3]

Jason McMartin has taught theology at Biola University for twenty years. As an urban missionary and bivocational pastor and church planter, he has served with Christians battling large-scale social problems such as poverty, immigration, and Covid-19 while navigating the day-to-day losses we all experience.

Though each of us has experienced suffering or walked closely with people going through hard times, we haven't based this book only on our experiences. Through the generous funding of the John Templeton Foundation and the Templeton World Charity Foundation, we've been doing interdisciplinary research for many years. In addition to Liz, Kelly, and Jason, our team included Crystal Park, a leader in the psychology of religion who developed the meaning-making model that we use throughout this book; Eric Silverman, a philosopher with expertise in the problem of suffering and a personal history with cancer; Jamie Aten, a specialist in disaster psychology who is living with stage four cancer; and Laura Shannonhouse, a professional counselor who has worked extensively with refugees and cancer survivors.

We have all contributed our expertise, seeking to understand how Christians draw on their faith when faced with life difficulties. Over the course of these six years, our research has included not simply reading academic books and specialized articles, but listening to people in diverse settings who have suffered. We have interviewed almost a hundred Christians from a variety of backgrounds with cancer diagnoses and also surveyed large samples of cancer survivors, refugees from ten language groups, people who'd lost loved ones, and survivors of natural disasters. Through carefully constructed interviews and surveys, we asked loads of questions and tried to listen well. We also studied, from a theological perspective, the rich resources Christianity offers those who suffer. Over time we have learned a great deal about how Christians rely on their faith to cope with suffering, as well as how these efforts relate to positive outcomes such as mental health and flourishing.

Through our years together, we have published dozens of research articles in peer-reviewed journals, but the truth is, most of the people who might benefit from what we learned will never see that academic work. We decided to remedy that situation by distilling what we'd learned into this book. Here we have blended together the best psychological observations and theological insights we could find, hoping to make them understandable and applicable for all of us.

We wrote this book primarily for people in the trenches—those who have encountered significant challenges on the road through life and are struggling to face these well. This book is also for companions: the husbands, wives, children, parents, and friends of people who are going through hard times, as well as pastors and counselors who so regularly enter into the suffering of those facing life's storms. It is often difficult to know what to say or do that is helpful. This book can equip you to be a better travel partner.

We hope that this book will pass on many of the lessons we have learned.

AN OVERVIEW OF THE ROADMAP

This book is a kind of roadmap. In some ways, your path will be completely your own since no one else has experienced your particular suffering—that is *your* story, although others play a part in it. Yet as you walk through suffering, our Christian faith offers signposts along the way, resources for finding meaning so that even the difficult path can be a means of grace. For your story is not simply your own, but also God's. He is present, active, and purposeful. Numerous biblical authors describe this path, providing guidance regarding your destination, places you may visit along the way, and practices for getting you through. We'll also discuss psychological research that will help settle some details of this roadmap. We hope you experience this book as a kind of companion as you go.

The end of each chapter will provide questions to help you think about the material you have read and relate it to your own experience. Some chapters also suggest specific exercises and practices that we hope you will incorporate into your daily life. Consider keeping a journal of your responses to the questions and experiences with the exercises. Research shows that when people deliberately work through their pain—sitting with their emotions, wrestling with why terrible things happen, and figuring out what it all means for their future—they come out better and stronger on the other side.[4] The key isn't just thinking about what happened, but approaching that pain with genuine curiosity and a willingness to find meaning in the mess.

We encourage you to work through the book with others. We were created for community, and our brothers and sisters in Christ can be a great help as we find new meaning and new ways of telling our story through the meaning-making process. The questions can serve as a guide for discussion and a starting point for telling your experiences, learning from each other, and receiving support as you grapple with the meaning of your journey.

A word about what you will find in this book: Chapters one to four provide a warning against problematic roadmaps, as well as possible destinations and ways of thinking about suffering (the "meanings" in the meaning-making model). Beginning in chapter five, we will cover seven Christian practices, one in each chapter, that can assist with the meaning-making process. These practices—including identification with Christ, lament, surrender, forgiveness, gratitude, remembering our mortality, and testimony—work together to accomplish the purposes of suffering as they help us rebuild meaning.

We are glad you have allowed us to be a companion on your journey. Whether you are reading this book for yourself or to equip yourself to help others, we hope you will think through the content and exercises we provide and that this book leaves you with a clearer sense of the journey ahead, a greater knowledge of the resources our faith provides along the way, and a deeper connection with our Lord Jesus Christ, who walked this path before us and now walks alongside us.

FOR REFLECTION OR DISCUSSION

1. We state that "getting past suffering involves going through it, not around it."
   - What has been your typical approach when difficult life events come your way?

- Do you tend to confront them directly or try to avoid them?
- How has your typical approach to suffering helped or hindered your ability to cope and grow through difficult experiences?

2. In this book we will emphasize the importance of intentionally processing your suffering. As you start to read—especially if you or someone you care about is currently dealing with suffering—we encourage you to set up a small support system. This can be as simple as asking a few people to read and discuss each chapter with you as a small group. Such a setting would allow you to start processing the material with others. Suggestions for structuring this group can be found in the appendix.

PART ONE

A ROADMAP FOR THE JOURNEY

ONE

SUFFERING AND MEANING

[After my diagnosis] I would say, "God, I'm not understanding this. Why is this happening?" I wasn't angry with God. I was confused. And I was looking to God to help me make sense of it.

John, cancer survivor

You know that moment when life stops making sense? When something happens that's so at odds with how you thought the world worked that you feel like you're standing on quicksand? Fredrich Nietzsche, perhaps the most famous of all atheists, once said, "The meaninglessness of suffering, and not suffering as such, [is] the curse which has hung over mankind."[1] If you have gone through a devastating life crisis—the loss of a loved one, an assault, an unwanted medical diagnosis—you may recognize the feeling of emptiness that often accompanies these events. In a moment, your world is turned upside down. Things that brought you satisfaction and purpose now seem pointless or shallow. Life feels meaningless.

In one way Nietzsche was wrong. Suffering is not meaningless in a world created and sustained by a loving God who is in the business of redeeming the world. But in another way, Nietzsche was right—he was right about how meaningless suffering can feel. It's like having the rug pulled out from under you, except the rug was actually the floor, and maybe the whole house. Your stomach drops. Your chest tightens. Nothing feels solid anymore.

Suffering challenges our ordinary ways of understanding the world and our place in it—our "meaning system," a kind of operating manual for life. You had a set of assumptions about how things work, guidelines you lived by, a story you told yourself about the world. Then circumstances hit you with something that didn't fit that story at all. Disorientation ensued.

To find our way out of suffering, we must begin rebuilding, sifting through the pieces of our devastated lives to rebuild our sense of meaning. We must figure out, again, in light of our new circumstances, what life is about, who we are, and what our place in the world is. Psychologists call this "meaning-making coping." The good news is that this disruption creates an opportunity for growth and even flourishing. But why is this the case? How can good come out of bad?

It is hard to overestimate the importance of meaning—that is, an understanding of one's place and purpose in the world—for well-being. Some psychologists even see the need for meaning as one of the main characteristics of being human. Suffering certainly illuminates the significance of meaning. Viktor Frankl, a psychiatrist who spent time in a concentration camp under Hitler's regime, described this perspective in his famous book, *Man's Search for Meaning*. He wrote, "He who has a why to live for can bear with almost any how."[2]

WHEN YOUR LIFE BLUEPRINT COLLIDES WITH REALITY

Psychologist Crystal Park's meaning-making model clarifies what happens when we encounter difficult life events that challenge our sense of meaning and how this can produce positive outcomes.[3] She describes the process of meaning-making coping, of rebuilding our meaning system after it has been challenged by hardship. In order to understand how this process works, we must first understand the difference between global and situational meaning.

Think about it this way: You've been living your life according to a blueprint—your assumptions about how the world works, what matters, where you're headed. Maybe you didn't even realize you had this blueprint until something happened that made absolutely no sense according to your plans. That blueprint is what psychologists call your "global meaning." It is the framework through which we evaluate all the events in our lives and that influences how we respond to those events. Our meaning structures direct every decision we make at every moment of our lives.

Sometimes we refer to global meaning as our "worldview." It consists of core beliefs about the world and our place in it, our life goals, and the feeling that life has meaning and purpose. And then life happens. But life doesn't just happen; we also interpret what's happening in a certain way. Our views on what's happening right now—this new, unwelcome reality—is what we call "situational meaning." It's our assessment of the specific event at hand: the job loss, the diagnosis, the betrayal, the accident.

Here's the crucial insight: The degree to which our view of what's happening conflicts with our life blueprint determines how much distress we will feel. In other words, if this specific event challenges or threatens the ways we understand the world, we will experience distress. The greater the distance between our view of what's happening now and what we thought was true about life, the more upset we will be. Much of this distress comes from the threat to our meaning system—our worldview. Life starts to feel meaningless and without purpose.

THE THREE PILLARS OF OUR LIFE BLUEPRINT

Our life blueprint—what psychologists call our "global meaning"—rests on three pillars. When suffering hits, it can shake any or all of them.

Core beliefs about reality. These include whether or not there is a God, what God is like, whether reality is just material or also includes spiritual elements, and whether our lives and the world have purpose or we invent purpose as we go along. These beliefs about the world strongly influence how we behave in the world. One study found that our global beliefs predict outcomes such as gratitude and life satisfaction more strongly than do our personality traits, such as extraversion or introversion.[4]

Maybe you believe the world is generally fair and good things happen to good people. Then your spouse—who's always been faithful, kind, and generous—gets diagnosed with early-onset dementia at fifty-five. Or perhaps you believe that if you work hard and play by the rules, you'll be rewarded. Then the company you've given twenty years to eliminates your position to boost quarterly profits. Suddenly, what you thought was true about how life works doesn't seem true at all.

Life goals. These are the high-level purposes that guide our behavior and that we pursue in everyday life. They include broad goals that are informed by our values, such as the kind of person we want to be, the kinds of relationships we want to have, and what we will invest our time in. Life goals are closely tied to our values. Philosopher Eleonore Stump calls them "the desires of the heart" that, when blocked, cause suffering.[5]

Think of the mother whose deepest goal is raising healthy, happy children—then her teenager attempts suicide. Or the man who's worked his whole career toward retirement with his wife, only to lose her to cancer six months before he retires. These aren't just disappointments; they're threats to the very purposes that have organized their lives.

A sense that life matters. This refers to the feeling part of our global meaning system. It includes our subjective feeling that life has meaning, that our life has purpose, and that we matter. Even when we aren't able to verbalize what life's meaning is, or what our life purpose is, these feelings are an important part of our sense of well-being.

Emotional stability is often the first thing to go when crisis hits. Even if we can still intellectually affirm our core beliefs and remember our goals, we might find ourselves thinking, *What's the point?* We had meaningful work to do, but we can't bring ourselves to do it. Food loses its taste. Activities that used to energize us feel hollow. It's not depression, exactly—it's the sense that nothing matters anymore.

WHEN WHAT'S HAPPENING NOW DOESN'T MATCH OUR BLUEPRINT

In contrast to our life blueprint, what we call "situational meaning" is much simpler—it's how we interpret what's happening right now. When stressful events hit, we instinctively evaluate: *What is this? How threatening is it? Can I control it? Why did this happen? What does this mean for my future? Is this job loss an opportunity to move into a different life calling or a threat to my very identity? Is a diagnosis of cancer compatible with my life goals, or does it disrupt those goals? Is pandemic-related sheltering in place a chance to spend more time with God or a devastating loss?* The same event can be seen in vastly different ways; our situational meanings can vary.

When difficulties hit, part of our suffering has to do with the event itself: When we lose someone, we feel grief; when we have been hurt, we feel anger. But if our assessment of this new event (situational meaning) conflicts enough with our usual assessment of ourselves and the world around us (global meaning), then in addition to the suffering directly associated with the event, we also feel tossed about and vulnerable to whatever unknown forces we may next face. The ground beneath our feet shifts. We are no longer sure of ourselves or the way our world works, a frightening experience indeed. The world as we knew it has disappeared. Depending on the situation, our very identity, our sense of who we are, may be challenged.

We're not just dealing with cancer or job loss or betrayal. We're dealing with the terrifying realization that our map of reality might be wrong. And if we can't trust our map, how do we know where we're going? How do we make decisions? How do we even get up in the morning?

WHAT DOES THE PROCESS OF MEANING-MAKING LOOK LIKE?

Let's walk through an example drawing on personal experience. In her own words, Liz tells us her story of trying to find meaning in the midst of a cancer diagnosis.

***

The word *cancer* has a certain existential weight to it. Whenever it shows up in movies or books, it's shorthand for "this person is going to die." I vividly remember the moment I received the news. I was about to get into my car to take my two sons to church for youth group when my phone rang. My doctor said, "It's cancer."

I don't remember feeling much, but for some reason, I hunched over as if someone had punched me, and tears started streaming down my face. I asked the questions I needed to ask and took notes of next steps. But inside, my world had screeched to a halt.

That first night was the worst. I lay in bed next to my sleeping husband, my heart hammering so hard I was sure it would wake him. Every few minutes I'd remember all over again: *I have cancer*. The panic would crash over me fresh each time. I kept thinking about my teenage sons—how could I leave them without a mother? How could I do this to my husband, make him a widower when he still needed me? I couldn't make sense of it. This wasn't supposed to happen to me. I was healthy—I ate well, exercised, took my vitamins. I was young, only in my forties. There was no family history. I kept replaying my life, searching for clues: Was it something I did? Something I didn't do?

But the confusion went deeper than medical questions. I believed in a loving God who was in control of my world. So how was this loving? How was allowing me to potentially die young—leaving my sons motherless, my husband alone—an act of love? I found myself wrestling with God in my morning prayers: *How is this good? They need me.* To my surprise, the cancer diagnosis revealed something I hadn't known about myself. Even though my theology said the world was broken and I was a sinner, somewhere deep inside I'd bought into the idea that the world was basically fair. That I was a good person. That good people who love God and try to do right deserve to have good things happen to them—a philosophy eerily similar to that of Job's counselors (see Job 4:7-8). Cancer happened to other people, people who didn't take care of themselves, people who were older, people who lived bad lives. Not people like me.

My life goals felt suddenly pointless. I had meaningful work to do—research to finish, articles to write, students to mentor. But what was the point if I was going to die? I'd sit at my computer, staring at the screen, unable to care about anything that had seemed so important just weeks earlier. The future I'd been working toward—watching my sons become men, growing old with my husband, maybe becoming a grandmother someday—felt like it was dissolving.

Here's what I didn't understand then: My life blueprint—everything I'd believed about how the world worked—was in complete collision with my interpretation of what was happening to me. My core beliefs (God is loving and the world is fair to good people), my life goals (live long, be a good mother and wife and scholar), and my sense that life had meaning were all crashing into this new reality: cancer, possible early death, shattered plans. There was an enormous gap between what I thought was true about life and how I saw what was happening to me. And that's exactly where the worst suffering lives—not just in the hard circumstances, but in that terrible space where nothing makes sense anymore.

But I didn't stay stuck there. Without even knowing there was a name for it, I began what psychologists call the meaning-making process—the slow, difficult work of rebuilding my understanding of life so I could make sense of what was happening to me. Much of this happened during my quiet time every morning. I'd spend about an hour reading books about cancer—both secular and Christian ones—memorizing Scripture, especially psalms, writing in my journal, and, above all, crying out my distress before God. I wasn't just trying to feel better; I was trying to understand. How do I make sense of this? How do I rebuild my understanding of life so that cancer and God's love can both be true?

It took time, but slowly my terror faded, and my life blueprint—my global meaning—began to change as my heart theology finally started catching up with my head theology. I was able to internalize a bit more that the world was broken and consequently not just and that I didn't deserve for only good things to happen to me, but anything good I received was God's gracious, unmerited gift to me. My ways of understanding suffering began changing as I realized I needed more robust ways of understanding God's loving purposes for my life and for the lives of my loved ones.

My understanding of what was happening—my situational meaning—was shifting, too. Instead of seeing the cancer only as a cruel threat, I started wondering: What if God allowed this into my life for reasons I couldn't see yet? What if this wasn't just destruction but also an invitation—to know him differently, to help others in ways I never could before? The gap was closing—not because the cancer went away, but because my understanding of both life and my situation had grown deeper, more complex, more true. The meaning-making process had changed both sides of the equation.

***

As Liz worked through this process of meaning-making, she gained deeper insights even in the midst of the stress of this new season of life. For one, her goals changed. Her scholarship had previously focused on gender issues, but now it became almost entirely devoted to the area of meaning-making in suffering. Sometimes the process results in character growth. For example, Liz experiences herself as more even-keeled since the cancer, as she's gained greater calmness and perspective. Facing her possible death has made it easier not to be overwhelmed when other struggles come her way. Nor is she as shaken by the suffering of others—she doesn't feel the urge to move away from their suffering in order to protect herself, as she might have done in the past.

HOW DO PEOPLE GROW THROUGH SUFFERING?

Moving through suffering requires that we rebuild meaning structures—what Crystal Park calls the meaning-making process—if we are to resolve the discrepancy between global and situational meaning.[6] Resolving this discrepancy can restore a view that the world has purpose and that life is worthwhile. It can also lead to growth. For decades psychologists have been fascinated by people who don't just survive terrible experiences but say their lives are better because of what they went through.[7] The research reveals something counterintuitive: The more our fundamental beliefs about life get shattered, the more room there is for profound growth. This transformation tends to happen in three connected ways:[8]

We see ourselves differently. People discover they're tougher than they ever imagined, but also more human. They report feeling both stronger and more accepting of their own fragility and finitude.[9] Many develop the kind of wisdom that comes only from having weathered real storms.[10] Increased patience and perseverance are also among reported positive character changes.[11]

Our relationships deepen. Suffering has a way of cutting through superficial connections. People find themselves valuing others more deeply, feeling more connected to fellow human beings, and developing genuine compassion for others.[12]

Our worldview shifts. The big questions about meaning, purpose, and what really matters get answered in new ways. What once seemed important may fade away, while previously overlooked aspects of life suddenly become precious.

We saw evidence of this in our interviews with cancer survivors. Greg said, "To me, what this cancer journey has done is it's changed my perspective. It's changed my perspective on what I want the last year, the last decade of my life, really, to look like. It's changed my priorities. . . . I always say, 'Watch where you spend your money, and I'll tell you what your priorities are.' I will tell you that I am probably spending less time on my career and more time on people and the relationships that matter to me."

Ginny similarly noted a change in perspective after her cancer. "I think it made me a lot calmer, a lot more accepting," she said. "I don't get as nervous or wound up about things as I used to. Because I've seen what real problems are. . . . It's like I have to go back to my faith and to where I belong, and the things that matter. And that's where I've landed, is I can separate what matters and what doesn't."

The meaning-making process helps us grow and enriches our lives when we engage with our suffering, drawing on our faith and its practices to reconcile our global meaning with our situational meaning.

Meaning-making can lead us to discard unhelpful or untrue beliefs and misguided goals and values, and to adopt a better way of understanding the world and our place in it.[13] For example, the simplistic belief that God won't allow any suffering to come to those who trust God may give way to the more resilient belief that suffering will come but can be redeemed by God. Even when global beliefs and goals are fairly solid, the meaning-making process can cause these to become more complex, nuanced, and internalized. Our faith is deepened and our trust in God grows. We see ourselves, others, and the world in a way that aligns more with the way God sees them—with love and compassion.

When we are able to resolve the discrepancy between our global and situational meanings through this reconstruction, our suffering can be incorporated into our life narrative in useful and informative ways. Psychological research suggests that the more complex and nuanced our global beliefs are, the better off we are. The more we incorporate our suffering into our life story, the more we will grow. When we see the world the way it really is, in all its complexity, ambiguity, beauty, and fallenness, we can live in that world in more true and productive ways. Simplistic ways of viewing the world and our suffering lead to conflict with reality, which tends to foster impoverished lives.

Nita, a cancer survivor in one of our studies, illustrates how she incorporated her cancer experience into her life narrative. She said, "I talk to people who've been newly diagnosed. I didn't want to at first, but now it feels like this is part of why I went through it—so I could help somebody else. And I don't give them medical advice, because I'm not a doctor. But I can tell them, 'This is what it was like for me. This is how I felt. This is what helped.' And I can see it in their eyes, this relief of talking to somebody who's been there. And that gives meaning to what I went through."

The research also shows that the meaning-making process can lead to poor outcomes. Helpful and true beliefs may be discarded and harmful ones adopted, leading to worse mental health. Linda, for example, entered counseling for help with her profound depression. Many years earlier, Linda's sister had been killed in a tragic accident. Linda was a Christian and even taught in her church's Sunday school, but her global system included the belief that God's goodness meant nothing bad would happen to people who believed in God. After her sister's death, Linda's meaning-making process did not result in a more nuanced view of God's goodness, providence, or intervention in people's lives, but in a loss of belief. She resolved the discrepancy between her global and situational meaning by giving up her faith. For her, a world where God did not exist was more easily reconciled with her sister's death.

Unfortunately, this meaning-making process also produced the depression that plagued Linda for many years. Given Linda's lack of faith, her decision to pursue counseling in a church-based counseling center may have unconsciously been motivated by a desire to find a more hopeful way of putting the pieces together. Only when she recognized that her unbelief was a way of expressing her anger at God and started letting go of that anger and unbelief did her depression begin to lift.

The process of meaning-making can affect any or all of our global meaning structures. If someone's concept of God implies that only good things happen to believers, then disasters can easily lead to the belief that there is no God. Similarly, people may discard important life goals without adopting new ones, leading to a sense of purposelessness. People can get stuck in the process and become unable to resolve the tensions, which leaves them in ongoing distress. In other words, suffering itself does not cause growth, as is sometimes simplistically assumed. Suffering may provide an opportunity for growth, but the quality and nature of meaning-making are what facilitate or hinder growth. It's a mistake to ignore the process of meaning-making and think that, as Christians, we need to jump to a triumphant place very quickly. The process needs time and care if it is to be beneficial, which requires allowing ourselves and others to invest that time and effort.

SUFFERING AND GLORY

The idea that suffering might lead to good things isn't new. After all, we see this throughout the Bible. God promises to work "all things" (including, one might assume, painful and traumatic experiences) together for good for those who love God and are called according to his purpose (Romans 8:28). This doesn't mean the "things" themselves are necessarily good—for example, it was evil that Joseph's brothers sold him into slavery (Genesis 37:12-36). But it does mean God remains faithful and active, bringing about good even through brokenness and suffering (Genesis 50:20-21). God will never compromise his holiness or love, and he will be faithful to his people, promising that their suffering is not the final word. Good can and will come.

Scripture describes these good outcomes by pervasively connecting suffering with the somewhat mysterious concept of "glory." Jesus interpreted his own suffering by referring to Old Testament prophecies, commenting, "Did not the Messiah have to suffer these things and then enter his glory?" (Luke 24:26). Reviewing these same prophets, Peter spoke of "the sufferings of the Messiah and the glories that would follow" (1 Peter 1:11).

The connection of suffering with glory also includes us, Jesus' followers. Peter tells us to "rejoice inasmuch as you participate in the sufferings of Christ, so that you may be overjoyed when his glory is revealed" (1 Peter 4:13). Paul picks up on this theme in 2 Corinthians 4:17, where we are told that "our light and momentary troubles are achieving for us an eternal glory that far outweighs them all." Elsewhere he writes that "we share in his sufferings in order that we may also share in his glory. I consider that our present sufferings are not worth comparing with the glory that will be revealed in us" (Romans 8:17-18).

What does *glory* actually mean? Does it mean fame or notoriety? That seems fairly base and shallow, not reflecting what we find in Scripture. The Hebrew Bible gives us a different conception: "Glory" (*kavod*) is rooted in weightiness and is picked up in the Greek New Testament as conveying honor (*doxa*). Glory can communicate not just the physical meaning of "heaviness" (though not in a burdensome sense), but also "the majesty or honor in human interaction" and "God's majesty or honor."[14] This glory is linked to God's presence, even linked to the revelation of his face (Psalm 24:6-10). In the Psalms and the prophets, *glory* was also used to refer to the vision of God's power and presence that will one day fill the earth, provoking worship and awe before our majestic God (Psalm 29; Isaiah 6, 40; Ezekiel 1). In the New Testament, God's glorious presence takes form in the person of Jesus (1 Corinthians 4:6), and these end-time prophecies become intertwined with Christ's second coming. Jesus is God's glory made clear, so now our glory is linked to our connection to this Messiah.

Clark, one of our participants with a cancer diagnosis, was attuned to this connection between his suffering and glory. He said, "You know, Lord, if you allow me to go through this, then you definitely have a purpose. And whatever that purpose is, is for your glory. And I know that you're going to take me through it and everything. So just keep on giving me your peace. You know, and that, that's just what I stood on." Tying his suffering to the purpose of giving God glory enabled Clark to have peace in a very difficult time.

The apostle Paul used *glory* to describe the believer's salvation. Specifically, the Holy Spirit shapes us to become more and more like Christ, culminating in our complete transformation at the time of Jesus' second coming. And this is where suffering comes in. According to the book of Philippians, becoming like Christ includes participation in his sufferings (Philippians 3:10) and in his resurrection (Philippians 3:21). In linking suffering to glory, Paul points out that suffering enables us to increasingly know and identify with Christ (including, significantly, with his suffering), to become conformed to Christ's image, and to anticipate our ultimate transformation into glorious Christlikeness. We will fully and securely be in God's presence, soaking up the rays of his shining face. While we must be mindful of the warning of idolatry, that we become what we worship (Psalm 115:4-8), the flip side reminds us of the goodness of becoming like the true and glorious God. As Paul puts it in 2 Corinthians 3:18, "And we all, who with unveiled faces contemplate the Lord's glory, are being transformed into his image with ever-increasing glory, which comes from the Lord, who is the Spirit."

Many of these themes were echoed by Christina, one of our participants, who discovered during her cancer treatment, "this journey means something. . . . I'm anticipating what this greatness is going to be. . . . I know how to dive now whereas I didn't; I know how to dive down into my quiet place and just start worshiping." From the Christian perspective, the hard road to the good life is the hard road to glory.[15] Will you accept God's invitation to journey with God through suffering to glory?

FOR REFLECTION OR DISCUSSION

1. A good starting point for meaning-making is to identify the places where your global and situational meaning—what you thought was true and what you are now experiencing—are in tension. In Liz's story above, this tension was between her understanding that God was good and the perception that her potential death from cancer would be devastating for her young sons. Here are some approaches to help you identify your global and situational meaning:
   - Psychologists call global beliefs about the world "primal world beliefs," or "primals." You can take a survey and receive feedback on your own primals at myprimals.com/discover-your-primals. While primal beliefs are only one part of your global beliefs, reflecting on the feedback you receive can help you understand your global world beliefs a bit more.
   - Emotions can help us uncover places where our global and situational beliefs are in tension. For example, Liz felt surprise at her diagnosis and realized that this revealed some mistaken beliefs in her global meaning system. Pay close attention to your varied emotional reactions. Sit with them and try to figure out what those feelings are about. What

automatic thoughts and physical sensations accompany those feelings? Do they tell you something about what you expected, based on your global meaning system? Do they tell you something about how you are perceiving your current situation, reflecting your situational appraisal? Do they help you identify places where you experience conflict, which might help you see where your global and situational meaning are in tension?

- Have a dialogue with yourself, between parts that hold conflicting beliefs or emotions related to your suffering. For example, imagine a conversation between a part that feels angry or betrayed by God and a part that trusts in God's goodness. Approach this exercise with curiosity and self-compassion, leaving aside any judgments.
- Global purpose is an important part of the global meaning system that is often blocked through suffering. To identify what your global purpose is, imagine you are at the end of your life, looking back on your journey. What would you want to have achieved? What would you want to be remembered for? What kind of impact would you hope to have made on the world and the people around you? Now reflect on how your global purpose is affected by your current suffering.

2. Lectio divina is an ancient practice intended to open our hearts to what the Holy Spirit is saying to us through the Bible. Throughout the book we suggest some passages for lectio divina. In this chapter we noted the connection between suffering and glory—here are two suggested passages for reflecting on this hard road to glory: Romans 8:18-23;

2 Corinthians 4:7-18. Briefly, here are the steps you will follow to practice lectio divina:

- Read the passage slowly and attentively, listening for a word or phrase that stands out to you.
- Meditate on this word or phrase, pondering its meaning and significance in your life.
- Pray, responding to God's invitation and allowing the Scripture to guide your prayer.
- Contemplate, resting in God's presence and allowing the Scripture to sink deeply into your heart.

3. The famous theologian R. C. Sproul once quipped, "Why do bad things happen to good people? That only happened once and He volunteered." What is your response to this quote? How does it challenge or confirm your global beliefs?

FURTHER READING

Ronnie Janoff-Bulman, *Shattered Assumptions: Toward a New Psychology of Trauma* (Free Press, 2002).

Viktor E. Frankl, *Man's Search for Meaning* (Beacon, [1946] 2025).

TWO

PROBLEMATIC ROADMAPS

I was taught, "God works it all out for good, so praise him in your troubles." And if you don't praise him through your troubles, you're missing the blessing. And so there was this expectation that I would just praise God through it all. And, I don't know, I don't think I met that expectation. I think I had my moments where it was a roller coaster. . . . I kind of almost felt like there was this implied "God is up there, and God has the power, and God has control over this. And if you're just good enough, he's going to come in and solve it."

Monica, cancer survivor

The Christians we've interviewed for our research show remarkable variety in the ways they've drawn on their faith to cope with suffering. Some of their stories reveal great theological depth and emotional intimacy with God.

Susy, a former missionary in her forties who dealt with family betrayal and sexual abuse in addition to cancer, expressed how God tenderly taught her many things through her suffering, which she in turn shares with others through her art. Janet, an elderly saint, teared up when trying to communicate her gratitude at all the ways her relationship with God became more intimate during her own cancer journey.

Others generally embraced God's purpose in their journeys but struggled to find real meaning or purpose. Some drew on their faith traditions in ways that seemed theologically problematic. John had a list of "healing verses" he read each day, believing that this habit guaranteed him continued remission from cancer. His faith functioned as a kind of magic ritual in which he could maintain the appearance of control over his cancer through this daily practice.

Steve's story revolved around seeing cancer as God's punishment, which he couldn't understand because he saw himself generally as a pretty good guy. The faith of our participants had much in common, but the stories they constructed around their cancer journeys differed vastly from each other.

MAKING MEANING

Psychologists who study how we make meaning tell us we create the stories of our lives by combining our thoughts and experiences with the meaning-making resources available to us. As researchers, when we tell people we study how Christians cope with personal struggles or suffering by "making meaning," they sometimes look puzzled and ask, "Don't you mean how they find meaning?" *After all*, they think, *Christians have access to God's truth through the Bible, so all they have to do is find God's meaning—not make it!*

"Finding meaning" would be the more accurate phrase if we understood our suffering solely through what the Bible says—but we don't! Our research, including interviews with almost a hundred Christians with cancer diagnoses, uncovered diverse approaches sincere Christians used to put together their cancer stories in ways that reflected many influences in addition to their faith, and sometimes in ways that were in tension with their faith. They "made" meaning instead of simply "finding" it.

Making meaning is something like planning a road trip, where we consult guidebooks and seek reviews about attractions. In the same way, our faith, culture, and families provide us with ideas and practices for how to travel through life. But our trips never go as planned. The must-see attraction may be closed or under renovation. Or we decide to take a chance on the quirky roadside museum and find a hidden gem. Delays, breakdowns, and faulty directions take us through unexpected detours, some of which are frustrating and some quite wonderful. The fog may obscure the breathtaking viewpoint. Because of all this, our trip ends up being a combination of advice from others and what our own needs, desires, and interests contribute to the experience. Our journey is unique.

Sometimes the materials available for creating our stories are not very good. Sometimes the ways of understanding suffering offered by our churches, faith communities, or culture are not substantial enough. Sometimes what they offer doesn't fit our circumstances. When we try to weave these inadequate pieces into our life story, the result feels deficient, empty, or incomplete, especially when it comes to our suffering—it doesn't have the structure that will help us arrive at a satisfactory conclusion.

Liz's breast cancer diagnosis threw her for a loop. She had no family history of cancer; she exercised regularly and ate decently. At forty-five she was still fairly young. Her stage two diagnosis seemed to come out of nowhere. Although her doctor gave her a good prognosis, Liz's own research indicated she had a one in five chance of being dead in ten years. She faced a situation for which she felt entirely unprepared, in spite of being a Christian her whole life, reading her Bible regularly, and even teaching in her adult Sunday school class. Contemplating the weeks and months ahead, she felt lost. She didn't know how to face the suffering well.

An avid reader, she started working her way through Christian books on cancer. She found some to be profoundly depressing, especially the stories of people who responded to their diagnoses with bravery and concern for others—and then died. After reading the harrowing stories of other Christians with cancer, her suffering by comparison seemed to lack validity, and worrying about a "mere" stage two diagnosis seemed shallow. Sometimes she ran into startlingly bad theology, such as a book stating that all Christians were promised healing (and that it was unfortunate that non-Christians didn't have the same guarantee).

Most of the books, however, simply felt irrelevant to her experience, going on and on about why God would allow suffering such as cancer. The abstract question of God's involvement in suffering did not bother Liz at that moment. Her focus was not on abstract questions; it was on the more immediate and concrete question of what she could do to get through this tough time. How could she cope with this life-threatening illness?

Our interviews with other Christians who have gone through suffering reveal experiences like Liz's. Her story underlines three problems we have identified consistently in the suffering roadmaps generally available: they are vague, they are triumphalist, and they are defensive. In this chapter we will address these three problems presented by mainstream conservative

Christianity when addressing the theology of suffering. To use our journey metaphor, we will explore the faulty roadmaps we use to navigate our suffering.

VAGUE ROADMAPS

Before we had the convenience of GPS guidance, we had to rely on paper maps to get to our destination. Often an invitation came with a handmade, not-to-scale sketch of how to get to the location. We can all probably remember passing a turnoff, or missing the supposedly impossible-to-miss sign on a building, and arriving late or not at all! Similarly, people who are suffering sometimes hear advice that is so general in its contours that it provides little real direction for what to do.

In our interviews with cancer patients, a verse that came up again and again was Romans 8:28: "In all things God works for the good of those who love him." This hope-filled verse is at the heart of a chapter packed full of rich materials for a theology of suffering. But the only roadmap some people could find or construct started and ended with this verse. Their only guidance was a promise that God would bring something good out of the suffering. That's it. That's the only thing they knew about suffering in the context of their faith.

To make matters worse, this verse can become twisted, even hurtful, used almost like a weapon against the person enduring pain. Would-be helpers often cite this verse in ways that unintentionally minimize the suffering of others. Their message seems to be that people going through hardship should just focus on the positive and get to work looking for those silver linings. Sometimes people interpret this verse as a simplistic, sentimental, unrealistic assurance that life will have a happy ending. This approach to suffering almost always produces disappointment or even despair, as well as loss of trust in God when the promised happy ending does not appear. What was meant as a comfort amid difficulties becomes almost like a taunt from God.

This verse can thus be misused as a reason to search for the "good things" promised or specific results produced by the suffering, such as a reconciled relationship or the opportunity to be a witness—anything that will make the suffering "worth it." But this attempt to understand suffering rarely takes the context of Romans 8 into account, and consequently, it leaves the interpretation of "good" up for grabs. Often the "good" is considered too individualistically. People assume "God works all things for the good" means "God works all things for *my* good." Sometimes misguided attempts to identify the precise good trivializes the suffering. Or the "good" seems disproportionately small in comparison to the suffering. Does gaining a bit of patience really outweigh the suffering of a chronic health condition? Does the opportunity to share Christ with a coworker merit the death of a child?

While God's promise to redeem our suffering is at the heart of the Christian view of suffering, that basic idea needs to be fleshed out into a much more detailed and useful roadmap if it is to provide the comfort and guidance we need. Deep suffering requires robust theology. One glaring omission from this vague roadmap is Jesus. How does God work all things for good *through Jesus?* As the Bible narrates, Jesus is at the center of a robust Christian story about suffering. He is the suffering servant, the one who took on himself our pain and suffering (Isaiah 53:4).

TRIUMPHALIST ROADMAPS

After her diagnosis, Liz felt cut off from "normal" people who were not living their lives in the shadow of cancer. One day she was checking out at the grocery store when the friendly cashier asked, "And how are you doing today?"

Liz briefly thought of saying she'd just been diagnosed with cancer and was afraid she would die—but thought better of it and simply responded, "Fine, thanks!" Going to church often felt this way, too. Although she appreciated the expressions of care from friends and acquaintances, the unrelenting positivity of the worship service contributed to her feeling of disconnection from people around her.

The Psalms—the hymnbook of the ancient Israelites—contain many songs that are oriented toward suffering and express pain to God. As many as 40 percent of the psalms are considered these "psalms of lament."[1] In contrast, not even 20 percent of the songs in three widely used contemporary hymnbooks express suffering. This avoidance of suffering in church contexts is widespread. Services tend to focus on bright and uplifting passages of praise and worship, skipping the harder verses. Our own testimonies of God's grace in our lives are usually wrapped up neatly, avoiding messiness and melancholy.

Similarly, our accounts of suffering jump too quickly to the end of the story. They ignore the process of arriving there, denying others a chance to hear about the potential for growth along the way and the rich biblical resources that are available to help address the process—not just the outcome!—of suffering. Roadmaps that focus only on the promised destination don't give much guidance for how to get there, nor do they tell us where we are. They may seem far removed from our own experience. The glowing descriptions in tourist guidebooks don't match the dingy reality. The fantastic vista may be there, but the fog of our present experience obscures it. Roadmaps that focus solely on Christ's triumph over death and suffering at the resurrection miss the long, hard road Jesus traveled to get there.

Cultural pressures perpetuate this faulty roadmap. We live in one of the most technologically advanced societies in the world. We use this technology primarily to maximize pleasure and comfort and avoid pain and suffering. We take pills to dull a mild headache or sore muscles. We avoid extreme temperatures by staying in our precisely heated and cooled homes. We avoid boredom by watching fast-changing images on a variety of screens, personalized to our individual tastes. We can even avoid reminders of illness and death by keeping the sick and elderly out of sight in places designed for their care, and confining death to hospitals and mortuaries. In this way, reminders of our fallen world are kept out of sight and out of mind. We are very, very successful at avoiding pain and suffering—until we aren't, and it crashes like an unwanted houseguest into our lives. Is it any wonder that society's goals of avoiding pain and gratifying desire spill over into our church contexts?

Living in a world marred by sin and brokenness means suffering is inevitable. Unless we prepare for suffering, it will catch us by surprise, and being ill-equipped will only amplify its difficulties. We do need our churches to remind us of Jesus' triumph over the grave, over sin and suffering. But if we exclude Good Friday and Holy Saturday from our understanding of Easter, this flattened vision of Jesus lacks relevance to the experiences of people who suffer. *If he is so victorious, why do I hurt so much? Why does he not rescue me?*

We need to be reminded that our Christ suffered both on the cross and in his everyday life. We need to be reminded that, until his second coming, Jesus is with us in our own suffering—indeed, he is in the heart of our suffering, and our suffering is in his heart. He doesn't just care about the destination; he is with us on the journey.

DEFENSIVE ROADMAPS

During World War II, the English took down all their road signs, milestone markers, signposts, and railway station signs. They expected the Germans to invade at any minute, and they made these defensive preparations so spies dropping from enemy planes would be unable to find their way. Of course, many good English people also got lost without the benefit of signage during these years! Defense was chosen over guidance.

Sometimes the roadmaps we are given for suffering similarly mislead us. When the topic of suffering comes up, many people assume that the most important (or only) question to address is why God would allow suffering. If God is loving, powerful, all-knowing, and just, why does suffering exist? This issue is often called "the problem of suffering," and the defense of God's actions and motivations is called *theodicy*. Many Christian books on suffering focus on this problem, providing a wealth of philosophical and theological arguments aimed at defending God's actions in allowing suffering. It is also often assumed that the most pressing question for people who are suffering is why God would allow this pain into their lives. But what if that isn't the most important question sufferers have? What if those answers are not even helpful for Christians who suffer? In that case, such books point people in a direction they hadn't asked to go. Consequently, many roadmaps people of faith offer to us aren't helpful for our specific circumstances. They guide us toward Dallas when we need to reach Los Angeles.

Our research, and that of others, suggests that many suffering Christians don't spend a whole lot of time wondering why God has allowed suffering into their lives (although this may depend on the nature of the difficult life event). Most are too busy figuring out how to get through the pain to ask why it's there. In fact, instead of doubting God's love, many people we interviewed (though not all) spoke movingly of experiencing God's goodness amid their suffering; instead of doubting God's power, they talked about a greater awareness that God was in control; instead of doubting God's existence, they experienced God as intimately involved in the details of their journeys.

Our research also confirms that theological attempts to justify God's goodness or existence in light of suffering don't address the needs of Christians in distress. We recruited a large online sample of practicing Protestant Christians who reported that they'd had a significant negative life event in the previous six months. We asked them about their views on some prominent theodicies, or defenses of God. We expected to find that the more people believed that God had good intentions in causing or allowing suffering, the better off they would be. Our results surprised us. Most of the associations were not significant. Believing more strongly that suffering was the result of humans' exercise of free will, for example, made no difference in people's experiences. In fact, a couple of theodicies made things worse. For example, the more people believed that God caused or allowed suffering to make us grow, the more post-traumatic symptoms they experienced.

In our interview studies, a few people did indicate that they struggled with whether God was justified in allowing such pain in their lives. Among the people who had resolved their struggles, the resolution took an interpersonal form: in humility, they acknowledged their dependence on God and surrendered their problems to him.

Why, then, is there so much emphasis in Christian writings on theodicy and why God allows suffering and so little focus on the nitty-gritty process of getting through it? It may be that modernity has persuaded us that understanding how the world works is the key to living in it. In ages past, the idea of mystery, of recognizing that we won't always understand what God is up to, was considered essential to understanding the world. Now there is far greater pressure to answer all questions and banish mystery. We are uncomfortable with the unknown or inexplicable. We want explanations, because when we can explain things, we think we can control them.

Since there is no universally accepted answer to the question of why God allows suffering (though there are many solid arguments that address it), nor a commonly agreed-on assumption that God's ways may be incomprehensible to us, we often feel justified in putting God in the defendant's box. We want him to answer our questions! We have shifted from wondering whether we are being judged by God to the belief that we are in a position to judge the Divine. While this sounds empowering at first, it often betrays our failure to realize just how little we know. Those who end up in the depths of suffering often discover the limits of their knowledge, and that relates to everything from the medical to the spiritual. The deeper they get, the less they feel they know. Mystery—and its accompanying humility before God—becomes pressingly relevant.

Theodicy may come up so often because it bothers the bystanders, the people who observe the suffering of others. When we see other people suffering, especially loved ones, we don't have the same concerns and experiences they do. We don't experience the pressing need to deal with the suffering itself, nor do we necessarily experience the comfort that can come from God during those times. We experience suffering from the outside, while they experience it from the inside.

Those who watch someone suffer often concentrate on concerns that the sufferer regards as less important—such as why they are suffering. Observers may assume that the crucial concern is whether the suffering is fair, but those experiencing pain don't have that luxury. Their focus is on getting through it. People who are drowning need a lifeline. Those who are swimming for exercise reject the lifeline because they wouldn't get any exercise if they used it. In short, we should aim to be pastorally sensitive to the needs of those who hurt. Many suffering Christians do not need explanations but guidance for how to take the next step.

Of course, some people who suffer do struggle with why God would allow that suffering. We don't intend to minimize the distress suffering people can experience when they wonder if God really cares, doubt whether God is powerful enough to intervene, or struggle with how unfair their suffering seems. Spiritual struggles of this type can make suffering even more difficult. Research shows that anger toward God in particular is associated with a number of negative emotional and physical problems.[2] If you are struggling with these issues, there are several good books available (some of which we recommend at the end of this chapter). Here we simply emphasize that focusing exclusively on defending God denies people the help they may need in finding their way through hard times. It also asks many of us to offer a theological account we are not equipped to give. While we may not have studied philosophical theodicies, we can all listen and offer the gift of our presence; we can witness the challenges and honor the sufferer's difficulty even as we might gently point them to God's compassion and grace. We don't need a graduate degree to do that.

In the following chapters, we do not directly discuss theodicy. Instead, our focus is on biblical guidance on suffering we may have missed: the "how" of suffering. Even in the book of Job, where Job is clearly asking hard questions about his situation and about God, God does not provide him with direct responses to his questions. Instead, God grants Job a powerful encounter with God that puts God's power, love, and faithfulness on display. As with Job, God normally answers us not with detailed explanations, but by being with us in our suffering through the incarnate Jesus.

A BETTER ROADMAP

Mark had faced several substantial challenges in his life, but the most recent was his wife's diagnosis with cancer. In an email he wrote to Liz,

> It is amazing to me how often warm, loving Christians try to rush things, as if the increasing effects of 12 rounds of chemotherapy were some sort of boxing match that my bride is consistently dominating. Actually, it is much stranger than that, because even a boxing match is a process. It's like so many friends want to reframe our suffering as

> a moment-to-moment series of knock-out punches delivered by my wife to cancer, prompting an endless stream of victory dances. A couple of days after the diagnosis, a friend texted me, "OK, ready for a mean verse? Philippians 4:4—Rejoice in the Lord always; again I will say, rejoice." . . . It feels to me that a triumphalist evangelical culture has affected the way we interact with our Bibles so that we see frenetic happiness as the mark of Christian maturity—as if being filled with the Holy Spirit is roughly equivalent to taking a high dosage of Adderall and Prozac at the same time.

We have a much better roadmap available to us than the one many Christians seem to follow. What we believe about God's nature and how he works in our lives makes a big difference in how we process suffering. If what we say we believe is clear and aligns with the experience of God's people in the Scriptures, and is accompanied by an open and trusting heart, we will be much better equipped to handle struggles of any sort. But if we depend on sentiment or the limited prejudices of our culture, and if we try to capture God within the bounds of our own tiny imaginations, we will get lost in our struggles.

Our roadmaps matter. When they are faulty, they risk misrepresenting who God is and how God is working in our lives and the world. Faulty roadmaps lead us to worse destinations. Psychological research demonstrates that when people hold roadmaps showing God as apathetic or unfair, they experience more depression and anxiety and experience life as lacking in purpose.[3] When suffering is seen as a demonstration of God's anger, people become increasingly distressed over time, in a kind of downward spiral.[4] When people think God's power over suffering is limited or that suffering is random, over time they tend to drift away from their faith.[5] But when people are convinced of God's love and power, they cope better and do better emotionally.[6]

The abundant biblical resources and rich theological traditions available to us can help us sketch out a roadmap to deal with suffering—or, if not a roadmap exactly, at least a daily itinerary. This may require us to get outside our own cultural and historical context. We can learn much from Christians throughout history who have faced persecution, wars, and natural disasters. People in the global church in parts of Asia, Africa, and South America face substantial difficulties on a regular basis and have much to contribute to discussions about suffering. In our own country, we can learn from brothers and sisters in the historically Black church, who have endured more than their share of suffering through slavery, emancipation, the civil rights movement, and the ongoing racial tensions of contemporary America. Theirs is a priceless help to others on this road. In the following chapters, we draw on these biblical and theological resources, as well as our own research, to highlight the road ahead and some paths for getting there.

FOR REFLECTION OR DISCUSSION

1. Consider the three common problems with theologies of suffering: vagueness, triumphalism, and defensiveness. Which of these problems have you encountered in your own experience or in your faith community? How have they impacted your ability to find meaning in suffering?
2. Reflect on a time when you received well-intentioned but unhelpful advice or support from others during a difficult

experience. What made their response feel inadequate or even hurtful? What kind of support would have been more meaningful to you?

3. Do you struggle with the problem of suffering? If so, spend some time with God around that issue. Write down your current understanding of why God allows suffering. Then, reflect on how this understanding has been shaped by your experiences, your faith community, and your cultural context. Consider how your theodicy might affect your ability to find meaning and hope in the midst of suffering.
4. Reflect on the following passages, using the instructions for lectio divina provided in chapter one: Psalm 139:1-18; Isaiah 55; Romans 11:33-36.

FURTHER READING

Richard Rice, *Suffering and the Search for Meaning: Contemporary Responses to the Problem of Pain* (InterVarsity Press, 2014).

Mark S. M. Scott, *Pathways in Theodicy: An Introduction to the Problem of Evil* (Fortress, 2015).

John Swinton, *Raging with Compassion: Pastoral Responses to the Problem of Evil* (Eerdmans, 2007).

THREE

CHOOSING BETTER DESTINATIONS

It's like I learned throughout this journey that tomorrow is not promised to us; we don't know. So here at this moment, only today. So we have to really try to do our best, do the best we can today loving each other, loving our family, our friends, our neighbor, even when we don't know them. We try to be the best version of ourselves with loving people, with sincerity, with genuineness. Because we don't know. We don't know about tomorrow.

Gina, cancer survivor

James was one of the first people we interviewed for our study with cancer survivors. Before his prostate cancer diagnosis in his mid-forties, he led, as he describes it, a classic upper-middle-class life in which he worked hard to provide his family with material things and spent the rest of his time focused on having a good time. Although he and his family attended church, his faith was not vital to him. He told us he lived "a very selfish kind of life" and was "very materialistic." But his diagnosis caused him to re-evaluate everything.

Desiring to abandon "a life of shallowness and selfishness," James wanted to live a life of "drawing near to God." In his mind, this meant focusing on fulfilling his God-given purpose of evangelism and discipleship. He started to notice a change in his treatment of others: "I try to show the love of Christ in my interactions." Although his cancer treatment has allowed him a few more years of life, his diagnosis is terminal. But he told us, "I don't live in fear every day. . . . I feel secure about where I'm going and what I'm doing, and my big prayer is that God gives me the time to complete the purpose that he's given me." James is writing an evangelistic novel, and his one prayer is that God would allow him to finish the book before his death.

If life is a journey, James's diagnosis led him to an abrupt change of direction. Rather than pursuing pleasure and getting more "stuff," he became focused on a different goal—a different destination. His story shows the dramatic shifts in purpose that can result from suffering. Destinations matter, because our everyday lives, whether intentionally or not, are aimed at certain outcomes and purposes. And not all purposes are equal, as we will explore in this chapter. If we dive deeper into James's narrative, we can tease out three interrelated strands of purpose, of destination. First, he has specific tasks he would like to accomplish, such as finishing his novel. A second strand involves living a life characterized by love—a broader, more pervasive goal. A third strand, lying in the background of these other two, has to do with increasing intimacy with God, which James perceives as his ultimate destination.

THE ROLE OF SUFFERING IN CHOOSING BETTER DESTINATIONS

Suffering can be an opportunity to redirect ourselves away from inadequate destinations and toward better ones. Several psychological studies have pointed to the same transition: People who have endured more suffering tend to report that life has more purpose.[1] God, in his goodness, can turn the evil of suffering to our benefit.

Not everyone makes such dramatic life changes as James. But many people report that suffering has changed their approach to life, bringing a shift in perspective. Things that mattered no longer matter. Neglected parts of life are now much more important. The destination—the place toward which our life is aimed—has changed. This happens for many reasons. For some, like James, the threat of death is a wake-up call. When death looms over us, the difference between what matters from an eternal perspective and what doesn't becomes much more striking. Suddenly, many of our preoccupations lose their appeal. C. S. Lewis describes this process in his own life:

> I am progressing along the path of life in an ordinary contentedly fallen and godless condition, absorbed in a merry meeting with my friends for the morrow or a bit of work . . . when suddenly a stab of abdominal pain that threatens serious disease, or a headline in the newspapers that threatens us all with destruction, sends this whole pack of cards tumbling down. At first I am overwhelmed, and all my little happinesses look like broken toys. Then, slowly and reluctantly . . . I try to bring myself into the frame of mind that I should be in at all times. I remind myself that

> all these toys were never intended to possess my heart, that my true good is in another world and my only real treasure is Christ. And perhaps, by God's grace, I succeed, and for a day or two become a creature consciously dependent on God and drawing its strength from the right sources.[2]

Some types of suffering make it impossible to participate in our previous activities. We become spectators of our own lives. And when we pull out of the scramble of the next activity, the next purchase, we get a glimpse of the big picture. This new perspective can be sobering, but it can also be inspiring. We can evaluate whether the life we are living is the life we want to live, or whether we have gone wrong somewhere along the way. We can choose to live differently.

For some of us, suffering shows us things that have been hidden even from ourselves. We may be mistaken about what is truly important to us, believing, for example, that we have organized our lives around following God and God's purposes for us, only to discover that we haven't. Our values and priorities become clear, for better or worse. We may find that our lives are really about making a name for ourselves or accumulating material possessions. Perhaps our days are filled with staring at little screens to find the next amusement. We may have been putting a lot of effort into avoiding pain! We may realize we do not live for grand purposes after all. Our suffering opens up an opportunity for us to reorient our lives to better destinations.

Lisa, one of the people we interviewed, underwent this transition during her cancer experience. She reflected on what she had learned: "You know, many, many people are very wealthy. Very wealthy, very successful. And so many of them are not happy and not at peace. . . . That's not where happiness or peace comes from. So now when I look at what a successful day is, it's being able to practice my faith. It's my family. It's those things that really matter."

LOVE: A DESTINATION WORTH PURSUING

Our beliefs about the meaning of life and what a good life looks like—the things that give our life purpose—are central to our global meaning system. We tend to orient our life, activities, and goals around living well or flourishing. Unfortunately, the individualistic and materialistic accounts of flourishing that predominate in Western culture can lead us astray. These accounts encourage us to find flourishing by looking within ourselves, deciding what will make us happy, and then orienting our lives around that destination.

Our picture of flourishing will deeply shape how we face our suffering. And many accounts of flourishing are completely devastated by adversity. Researchers have long been puzzled by the fact that the nations reporting the highest levels of happiness and life satisfaction are also the nations with the highest suicide rates.[3] Countries such as Denmark, Iceland, and Canada have extensive welfare benefits, low corruption, and well-functioning governments. People living in these countries have a high degree of freedom to pursue their own goals. So why do they also have high rates of suicide? Although research is inconclusive, the answer may lie in the kinds of flourishing people in these countries tend to pursue. These countries have very low rates of religiosity. The absence of God from their global belief systems deprives them of anchors that transcend the worldly elements of life, so the loss of physical well-being, meaningful employment, or relationships removes their strongest anchors. These goals and life purposes are all vulnerable to worldly mishaps and can disappear in a moment.[4]

What we need is a vision of flourishing that is grounded in reality, shapes everyday life, and yet can weather negative life events. The Christian vision of flourishing provides this. Our faith can withstand suffering and even thrive in hard times. And love is what orients this enduring Christian vision of flourishing.[5] The apostle John doesn't say, "God is loving." No, he puts it more forcefully: "God is love" (1 John 4:8). And just in case his readers didn't hear him the first time, he repeats this just a few verses later (1 John 4:16). All of 1 John 4 defines God as love and insists that love will be the primary characteristic of Christians who truly know God. But we don't just have to take John's word for it. Jesus himself placed love front and center. When asked what the greatest commandment was, Jesus talked about love: loving God and loving your neighbor.

Christian thinkers throughout the centuries have consequently placed love at the center of their vision of the truly human life, or what we might call the truly flourishing life. For example, the great African theologian Augustine, writing in the fifth century, regularly quoted Romans 5:5: "The love of God is shed abroad in our hearts by the Holy Ghost which is given unto us" (KJV). He used this verse to tie together all of history, from creation to Christ's second coming, and to frame our relationships with God, with others, with ourselves, and with the earth.[6]

Following Augustine, we can say we experience Christian flourishing to the extent our relationships with God, neighbor, self, and the rest of creation exemplify love: divine love received, participated in, and then extended to others.[7] Unlike secular versions of flourishing, love orients us toward each other, overcoming the self-focus of most visions of flourishing. Jesus comments that "whoever wants to save their life will lose it, but whoever loses their life for me will find it" (Matthew 16:25).

What makes the Christian vision of flourishing able to withstand any kind of suffering? It is not bounded by the timeline of our life on earth but extends into life everlasting. Our growth into love doesn't end with our death. Our horizon is broader, our future bigger and better than this life, extending into a life of flourishing without suffering. In C. S. Lewis's evocative words in the last book of the Chronicles of Narnia, our future is "further in" and "further up."[8] To assume flourishing starts and ends in this life, as is so common, means the end of the story is always negative. Eventually everyone dies. Because of the fall, things are not the way they were created to be. Circumstances often thwart the limited purposes we have for our present life.

In Ecclesiastes, the Preacher (thought to be Solomon) systematically explores several visions of flourishing "under the sun"—that is, in the limited timeline from our birth to our death. He lists the pursuit of learning and wisdom, the pursuit of pleasure, and the pursuit of wealth and achievement. He concludes that these are ultimately "meaningless." Fortunately, Solomon does not stop there but provides us a glimpse of life "above the sun" in eternal life with God, noting that God has put eternity into every person's heart (Ecclesiastes 3:11). He ends his book by giving the bottom line: "Fear God and obey his commandments, for this is what it means to be human" (Ecclesiastes 12:13 ISV).

Learning, wisdom, pleasure, and achievement all have their place. But by themselves they don't lead to flourishing. They can never fully satisfy. They are not good ultimate destinations. But when they are received as gifts from God and used for God's loving purposes, they can be experienced as guideposts to something greater. They give us tastes of God's goodness we can pass on to others in an abundant life filled with love. Again, to quote the Preacher, "A person can do nothing better than to eat and drink and find satisfaction in their own toil. This too, I see, is from the hand of God, for without him, who can eat or find enjoyment?" (Ecclesiastes 2:24-25). All these things are intended only to point us further on, to the source of ultimate flourishing: God.

Suffering can be the hard road to the good life, the hard road to glory. But this road requires us to make choices. It requires that we face not only our limitations but also our sins and shortcomings, calling us to turn to God in surrender. It involves giving up some of our deep-seated assumptions about ourselves and the world, such as the conviction that this present world can ultimately satisfy us, that we deserve only good things to happen to us, and that we are in control of our lives. But when we are willing to have our eyes opened, even by suffering, to see reality for what it is, we can move forward into the abundant experience of God's love that is prepared for us. We are promised that nothing—including trouble, hardship, famine, nakedness, or danger—can separate us from the love of God that is in Christ Jesus our Lord, the foundation of all flourishing (Romans 8:35-39).

LOVING GOD

The Christian vision of flourishing begins with experiencing God's love. And suffering can increase our capacity to know and experience God's love. It is not only in the absence of difficulty and trial but also in their presence that we can grow in our ability "to grasp how wide and long and high and deep is the love of Christ, and to know this love that surpasses knowledge," as Paul so eloquently puts it in Ephesians 3:18-19. The road through suffering has a destination, which is to experience God's love more fully. While it may surprise modern believers, many Christians through the ages—including Augustine, C. S. Lewis, Simone Weil, and others—have seen suffering as a kind of shortcut to knowing the depth of God's love. How can that be?

Opening ourselves up to experience God's love has several dimensions. It requires that we be present to God, giving God our full attention. It also requires a sense of trust in and closeness to God in which we vulnerably reveal tender or private parts of ourselves to God and experience God's loving response. Over the long run, it requires what the biblical authors call "abiding in God" or "remaining in God."

Although we want to experience God's love, we may experience some challenges in doing so. To begin with, we are finite and God is infinite, which means God will always be at least partly incomprehensible to us. God is God, and we are not. Mystery will always be present in our relationship with the triune God. Second, our intimacy with God will be influenced by our particular personalities. Some people possess more skills than others at interacting in ways that lead to intimacy. For example, a well-established finding in psychology shows that atheism is more common among people with an autism spectrum disorder (ASD).[9] The explanation for this seems to be that people with ASD have difficulty in mentalizing, which is the ability to infer mental states in others—what others believe, know, feel, and desire—and in empathizing, which involves feeling with others and attempting to take their perspectives. Even people without ASD vary in their ability to do this. Since God does not usually present himself to our awareness in bodily form, difficulty with mentalizing and empathy may also be a barrier to awareness of God.

Third, and most importantly, sinfulness hampers our loving relationship with God. We hide from God rather than opening ourselves up to divine presence. This pattern of trying to hide from God's nearness started in Genesis 3, where Adam and Eve hid from God because they were ashamed. Sometimes we do not really want to be close to God because we fear God's holiness or because God's moral perfection makes us more aware of our own failings. Sometimes we do not want to be aware of God's presence because we prefer our own ways and choices. Or we may cling to a kind of perfectionism in which we want to fix ourselves before we open ourselves up to God—a kind of prideful attempt at saving ourselves through our own efforts.

In other words, even when we know that God fully accepts us and we can be secure before our heavenly Father, our concepts, emotions, values, and manner of life often constitute barriers to intimacy with God and therefore need to be straightened out. We sometimes call that straightening process "sanctification." We have sinful habits of wanting our own way and not God's, of pursuing instant gratification rather than our long-term good in Christ. Even as creatures who are reconciled with God, we are internally fragmented, wanting what God wants but also often wanting something other than God's good. Paul describes this ambivalent state in Romans: "For what I want to do I do not do, but what I hate I do" (Romans 7:15).[10] Not willing what God wills becomes an obstacle to experiencing the rich depth of intimacy into which God invites us.

Suffering, oddly enough, can help us overcome these barriers. Although some people turn away from God when they encounter suffering, many others report startling experiences of God's love. Kate Bowler, historian at Duke Divinity School, recounts her story of being diagnosed at age thirty-five with stage four cancer, recalling an experience that for a time she felt uncomfortable telling anyone: "It seemed too odd and too simplistic to say what I knew to be true—that when I was sure I was going to die, I didn't feel angry. I felt loved." She discovered she wasn't alone. Augustine called it "the sweetness." Thomas Aquinas called it "the prophetic light."[11]

Similar experiences showed up in our interviews with cancer survivors. One older woman said, "[The cancer] was a turning point in my life, and it drew me closer to God. . . . It wasn't that I wasn't close, but your relationships grow, and they get more intimate. . . . I'm not glad that I went through it, but I'm just so glad that he was with me and that I'm here today because of him. You know, I trust him; I lean on him. . . . He's my all; he's my everything. I'm just so grateful." In further attempting to describe her experience of these changes, she said, "It's deeper, you know. And it's better. And I think—I think I hear him. I think I hear him more. I think I can be still in him and I can hear him clearer and be more discerning when it's him."

These words beautifully exemplify the parts of intimacy we have described: being present with God, being close to God, and abiding in God.

Why does suffering facilitate this kind of experience with God? At the most basic level, suffering prompts us to turn to others, including God, for comfort. It facilitates awareness of God, making us present to the God who is always present to us. Brother Lawrence said, "God is often (in some sense) nearer to us and more effectually present with us, in sickness than in health."[12] God is always with us, but he is more "effectually present" because we are more focused on God.

Suffering also causes us to pour out our hearts to God, often in very raw, honest ways, which enables closeness with God. Maria, one of our participants, expressed this with respect to her cancer journey, saying, "I'm just so glad that I've gotten through this to know him better, because I have somebody that I can just tell anything to and see that he's always there. And I think I'll always say in my prayer, just, 'Lord, thank you for loving me unconditionally. There are no conditions on your love for me; you just love me the way I am.'"

Edith, another participant, said, "[My cancer experience] drew me closer, because it was like, 'It's you and me, God,' you know? And I knew that he was always there, whatever it was that was needed, was just to be there. And sometimes I would tell him, 'Lord, just let me feel your arms around me, just let me feel you holding me.'"

Suffering also brings us to the end of ourselves, forcing us to face the limits of our control and our ability to change our circumstances. In this way, suffering makes it more likely we will turn to the one person who is in control and does have the power to help our suffering—God. Through recognizing our own limitations and our awareness of God's character, we can surrender to God. We can yield our will and our desires to God in a loving and active manner. Suffering, in this way, becomes a kind of shortcut to intimacy.

Together these experiences allow us to experience God's love in the form of connection described as "abiding in God" or "remaining in God." In John 15, Jesus uses an image of a vine with branches, in which the branches "abide in" or "remain in" the vine. The image depicts unity and interconnectedness. We remain in Jesus, and Jesus remains in us! Later in the passage, Jesus speaks of "remaining in my love" and ties the "remaining" back to God and connects the whole to obeying Jesus' commandment that we love one another. We follow Jesus in an atmosphere of being loved by God, loving him, and loving each other.

From a psychological perspective, this interconnectedness sounds like an experience psychologists call "intersubjectivity," a foundational component of human intimacy.[13] Intersubjectivity occurs when people transcend their own sense of themselves as individuals, as when two people share a common ground of understanding based on their joint experiences. When two people connect this way, they experience the world as "us" instead of as "me and you." They experience a kind of closeness in which the boundaries between "me" and "you" become more blurry—the desires, opinions, and preferences of the other person are experienced in some way as being part of themselves.[14]

Philosopher Eleonore Stump points out that, in relationship to God, there is an even more profound intersubjectivity than is possible with other humans, namely, in God's "indwelling" in the person of the Holy Spirit. According to Stump, this indwelling allows intersubjectivity to progress to a sharing not just of mental states, but of persons. What is shared is not just another person's thoughts or affect but the other person themself! This intimacy does not constitute a merger; the person does not take on, for example, God's omniscience, nor does the person lose their own self, mind, or will. In Stump's description of this state, the person "will be aware of the Spirit's mind within her own, and there will be shared mind-reading and empathy between them so that there is a kind of intimacy between them that surpasses what would otherwise be available to [the person] alone or in union with another human being."[15]

Two psychological studies have examined intersubjectivity with God.[16] One found that people who have a relationship with God develop the same kind of self-other overlap with God that people experience in close relationships with each other and that those with a more committed relationship to God show increased overlap. Another study demonstrated that evangelicals rated themselves as experiencing more intersubjectivity with God than both atheists and non-evangelical Christians.

Psychological research helps us understand some results of experiencing intersubjectivity. For example, couples who experience greater intersubjectivity don't just feel closer—they also report greater relationship satisfaction and are more committed to each other.[17] Research shows that experiencing intersubjectivity with someone else leads to what is called "expansion of the self." Their strengths start to feel like our strengths. Their perspectives become part of how we see the world. We begin to carry pieces of them within us—not merely in some mystical sense, but in measurable ways that psychologists can study. People who experience intersubjectivity report feeling more capable, more confident, and more equipped to tackle challenges they never thought they could handle.[18] Being connected to someone in this profound way doesn't just make us feel less alone—it makes us more than we were before. We become larger versions of ourselves, enriched by the qualities and wisdom of those we've connected with most deeply. The research suggests that intersubjectivity expands us in ways we never expected.

Similarly, we find that the connectedness described by Jesus in John 15 also results in taking on Christ's characteristics in a way that empowers us. Jesus speaks of bearing fruit and passing on his love to others. When we experience intersubjectivity with Jesus, we are empowered to do what Jesus wants us to do.

Paul speaks frequently of being "in Christ" (see, for example, Ephesians 1). This language indicates a change in our fundamental being so that union with Christ in his death and resurrection affects not just our salvation but also how we should live.[19] Being in Christ transforms us to become more like him (Philemon 2:5).

The biblical passages on abiding in Christ and union with him help us appreciate intersubjectivity. Someone who is intimate with God cares about and is intentionally attentive to the things God cares about. God loves all creation, especially humans, who are made in the divine image. Being intimate with God means seeing others as God sees them, with eyes of divine love. Those intimate with God are also aware of God's attentiveness to their own thoughts and activities. Experiencing intersubjectivity with God, in short, involves seeing the world as Christ sees it. Intimacy with God is characterized primarily by feeling loved. And, as Jesus described in the metaphor of the vine and the branches, this experience of being loved overflows into loving others.

LOVING OURSELVES AND LOVING OTHERS

Consider how exuberantly Paul talks about God's love in Ephesians 3, where he prays that his readers, "being rooted and established in love, may have power, together with all the Lord's holy people, to grasp how wide and long and high and deep is the love of Christ, and to know this love that surpasses knowledge—that you may be filled to the measure of all the fullness of God" (Ephesians 3:17-19). God's love is so overwhelming that people have to develop their capacity for it over time as they experience God's love more and more! Then we share that love with others.

Our love for others flows out of the love we have received from God. Our experience of God's love frees us to love others well, as we are able to do so wholeheartedly, leaving aside self-interest for the sake of the other. One of the ways God's love frees us is when we internalize God's attitude toward us: God's kindness, understanding, and acceptance. Psychologists study this attitude toward ourselves in the form of "self-compassion," a stance of being supportive toward oneself when experiencing suffering or pain.[20] We are able to have compassion for ourselves when we have received compassion from trusted and stable relationships—such as the relationship God offers us.[21] God understands our limits. As the psalmist puts it,

> As a father has compassion on his children,
> so the LORD has compassion on those who fear him;
> for he knows how we are formed,
> he remembers that we are dust. (Psalm 103:13-14)

God also showed his compassion for our sin and suffering in sending Jesus to rescue us from these effects of sin. God is compassionate toward us, and we grow in our ability to pass on God's love when we take in God's compassion and love for us.

Research indicates that our compassion for others is related to our compassion for ourselves; we are better able to love others when we have internalized God's love for us.[22] Self-compassion is crucial during times of suffering.[23] Generally, people who have self-compassion report less anxiety and depression and greater flourishing. They also recover better from negative life events. When we perceive we have failed, when we bump into our limitations, and when we are suffering, self-compassion allows us to cope more effectively with our own pain, to reach out and get the help we need, and to feel connected to others who are also suffering. During difficult times we are often unable to do the things we normally do. Tasks pile up, balls get dropped, and we may experience frustration at our limitations. Here we can remind ourselves of God's kindness toward us and practice experiencing the same for ourselves.

God's compassionate orientation toward us liberates us to express healthy self-compassion: It would be completely inappropriate for us to be more demanding and less forgiving than God. We should strive to never be less compassionate than God, including when that compassion is meant to be directed not merely toward others but toward ourselves.

When we experience God's love, it transforms us and allows us to love others. It even allows us to appropriately love ourselves. Suffering provides the conditions for us to experience God's love more fully. If suffering is a journey, then experiencing God's love is the destination. And once we are fully planted in that love-centered vision of the flourishing life, we can flourish even in the midst of suffering. Nothing can separate us from God's love, which is in Christ Jesus.

FOR REFLECTION OR DISCUSSION

1. Take a few minutes to fill in the blank in the following sentence. Jot down ten things you try to do every day. Be as honest as possible with yourself, and don't read the rest of

these instructions until you have completed this task: "In my daily life, I typically try to ________________________."[24]

2. Now go back to your list and put a checkmark beside the answers you feel are connected to loving God, loving others, loving creation, and loving yourself. Life is the accumulation of the things we do each day. Looking over what we strive for each day provides an honest glimpse into what we think is important and our life's purpose. What do your daily strivings tell you about your vision of the good life? Do you seem to be devoting your efforts to everything but the things you care about most deeply? What can you strive for in your daily life that would lead to true flourishing?
3. Using lectio divina, reflect on Luke 10:25-37 and 1 John 4:7-19.
4. Read the following quote by C. S. Lewis, then reflect on these questions: What do you love and how has it shaped you? Have you offered your loves to God?

> To love at all is to be vulnerable. Love anything, and your heart will certainly be wrung and possibly be broken. If you want to make sure of keeping it intact, you must give your heart to no one, not even to an animal. Wrap it carefully round with hobbies and little luxuries; avoid all entanglements; lock it up safe in the casket or coffin of your selfishness. . . .
>
> We shall draw nearer to God, not by trying to avoid the sufferings inherent in all loves, but by accepting them and offering them to Him; throwing away all defensive armour. If our hearts need to be broken, and if He chooses this as a way in which they should break, so be it.[25]

5. Set aside fifteen to twenty minutes each day this week to practice being present with God. Find a quiet place where

you can minimize distractions. Begin by taking a few deep breaths and inviting God's presence. Then simply sit in silence, focusing your attention on God's love and nearness. If your mind wanders, gently redirect your thoughts back to God. Close your time with a prayer of gratitude.

6. Take some time to reflect on any areas of your life where you may be hiding from God or where sin has caused internal fragmentation. Write a letter to God, honestly expressing your thoughts, feelings, and struggles. As you write, imagine God listening to you with compassion and understanding. Close your letter with a prayer of surrender, asking God to help you overcome these barriers to intimacy.

FURTHER READING

C. S. Lewis, *The Four Loves* (Harcourt, Brace & World, 1960).

Henri Nouwen, *The Return of the Prodigal Son* (Doubleday, 1991).

Cindy Bunch, *Be Kind to Yourself: Releasing Frustrations and Embracing Joy* (InterVarsity Press, 2020).

Brother Lawrence, *The Practice of the Presence of God*. Originally published in 1962, it's been republished by a number of different publishers since then.

Ruth Haley Barton, *Invitation to Solitude and Silence* (InterVarsity Press, 2004).

A. W. Tozer, *The Pursuit of God* (Christian Publications, 1948).

Andrew Murray, *Abide in Christ*. Originally published in 1864, it's been republished by a number of different publishers since then.

Kyle Strobel and John Coe, *Where Prayer Becomes Real: How Honesty with God Transforms Your Soul* (Baker, 2021).

FOUR

PURPOSES FOR SUFFERING

I feel, honestly, a lot more equipped to help people through really hard life situations. . . . I just feel, now that I'm on the other side of it, more equipped to come alongside someone, sit in the pain and the hard stuff with them. Because I know that's valuable, just to have someone be there who gets it. And I feel like cancer broke me open and gave me a vision for that, a vision to see that there's pain all around that needs to be acknowledged and not fixed.

Susan, cancer survivor

C. S. Lewis is most famous for his children's books about the fictional land of Narnia. But he considered his last work of fiction to be his most mature novel, a lesser-known book titled *Till We Have Faces*. This story, set in a barbaric ancient civilization, follows one woman's journey from internal fragmentation to wholeness.[1] The main character, Orual, isn't just unattractive—she is ugly! Her face symbolizes her ugly soul, which is marked by destructive bitterness and jealousy. Her ugliness is also reflected in the destructive god she worships, who is described as having no face and a thousand faces—an image of fragmentation. Orual's suffering eventually leads her to learn to put others ahead of herself, and the story culminates in an encounter with the gods. There Lewis puts in the mouth of his protagonist a profound question: "How can [the gods] meet us face to face till we have faces?"[2] At the end of the story, the gods resolve Orual's fragmentation and grant her a face of great beauty in a face-to-face encounter with God, the source of all love and beauty.

First Corinthians 13:12 tells us we now see God only in a limited way, but one day we will see God face to face, knowing and being known in a relationship of perfect intimacy. In the meantime, we can move toward deeper communion with God. Although counterintuitive, suffering can provide an opportunity for such increased closeness. Here we consider some ways in which suffering can help heal the fragmentation that is a barrier to our intimacy with God. God faithfully uses our suffering to reshape our "faces" so that we, too, can ultimately see God face to face.

ORIGINS AND DESTINATIONS, CAUSES AND PURPOSES

A life of intimacy with God is our ultimate purpose. God has a variety of means to bring this about that also redeem our experiences of suffering. Before we discuss some of God's purposes in our circumstances, a clarification is necessary. We must carefully distinguish between the *cause* or origins of suffering and the *purposes* of suffering. They are not the same. Causes have to do with *where the suffering came from.* Purposes are about *where the suffering is going and what God is doing with it.*

Theodicy considers where suffering came from within God's world and the role God may have had in its origins. While God did not create sin, evil, or suffering, God is the Creator, Sustainer, and sovereign Lord (James 1:13; 1 John 1:5). Determining how these pieces fit together occupies considerable attention among theologians and sometimes in our own journeys as believers. However we navigate these tricky debates, we must remember that God's role in "causing" or "allowing" suffering, while a problem for some, is not the primary question for most Christians going through a hard time.

For most of us, the distinction between causes and purposes can sometimes get blurred, because some of the most common causes that have been proposed also involve purposes. For example, the "soul-building theodicy" states that God causes or allows suffering in order to develop people's character. Believing that God can bring character growth out of suffering does not necessarily require God's role in causing or allowing suffering. Whether or not God had a direct hand in bringing about the suffering, it remains true that God can take our suffering and do something with it; he can make it meaningful by using it to bring about growth.

God causing or allowing suffering is not the same as God having a purpose for our suffering. For example, Jason has a friend who loves gardening. This friend has turned all kinds of abandoned objects into flowerpots: a rusty children's wagon, a worn-down tire, and so forth. These objects weren't designed to be flowerpots, but where others see trash, he sees an opportunity. He turns them into quirky, beautiful, useful objects that provide pleasure to those who see them.

It's not easy to answer why God allows suffering (its cause), but we do know that God is in the business of repurposing our suffering. Just as Jason's friend turned a child's wagon into a flowerpot, God can creatively redeem our pain and difficulties. This is different from saying God allowed suffering *so that* these purposes could be fulfilled. We should not confuse the cause of suffering with a purpose it can eventually serve, because it usually isn't helpful to believe that the cause of the suffering (why it happened) was to fulfill that specific purpose. Plus, we don't want to make God dependent on suffering, as if the only way he can work is in and through our pain. No, we must always keep in mind we are navigating these theological problems in a fallen and broken world, not a sinless world free of tears, shame, and anxiety. Our suffering can accomplish many good goals, but we should avoid saying that is why it's in the world in the first place.

Experiencing our suffering as having a purpose can be very helpful to us in coping with the challenge. In one of our studies, we interviewed thirty cancer survivors from a large congregation on the West Coast about how they drew on their faith throughout their diagnosis and treatment. Purpose emerged as an important theme.[3] People cared deeply about whether God had a purpose for their suffering. Imagining this was all for nothing was crushing, but having confidence in God's wisdom, grace, and ability to bring about good brought needed courage and hope. This isn't the same as believing that God wanted their suffering and delighted in their pain because God had a purpose. Testimony from these believers was not focused on the cause of suffering. Instead, people wanted God to redeem their suffering—what was God doing with it? Whatever the cause or source of their pain, would their suffering be "wasted" or "meaningless"? May it never be so. Affirming God and his purposes did not seem to undercut people's agency but instead empowered and sustained them in it. These participants drew on their experiences of suffering to construct a new or refined sense of purpose in life that was deeply informed by their own suffering.

GOD'S PURPOSES: KNOWN AND UNKNOWN

Well-intentioned but ill-advised people sometimes try to point out all the things God is accomplishing through our suffering. This is rarely helpful! God has intricate and eternal plans that are way above our heads. Way above our pay grade! What happens if we "explain" someone's suffering by pointing to something wonderful like a friend's conversion that seemed to come about because of our suffering, only to have that convert give up their new faith a year or two later? And even if they don't, it doesn't help "explain" our grief. We are not privy to all the whys and hows of life, especially in terms of explaining how suffering relates to God's purposes.

Years ago, Kelly worked with a college student whose father had been killed in an automobile accident while she was not living at home. Her family found itself overwhelmed with grief, unexpected questions, and loads of pain. They didn't need people to find the silver lining or explain to them why God "did this"; they needed the courage to believe that God had not abandoned them, that he wasn't cruel, and that even in the darkest mystery, he hadn't stopped being God. He was still working, still present, still able to bring hope and promise—but not by canceling out their grief, questions, and hurt. No; he was meeting them amid it. In humility we need to acknowledge that we may not know what God is up to in our suffering, but we can know he is present and filled with compassion and care. Furthermore, we can be comforted to know that God does have purposes, even if we don't know what they are.

Sometimes God does allow us to discern his purposes in our suffering. For example, Joseph in the Old Testament suffers a series of disastrous life events, including being sold into slavery and unjustly imprisoned. Later in the story, he nevertheless reflects that those trials have been used by God to put him in a position to save an entire nation from famine (Genesis 50). This doesn't mean the injustice was good, but it does mean he was never abandoned by God and that even amid pain and disappointment, God was working for good.

Similarly, Liz felt clearly from God that part of the purpose of her year in cancer treatment was to shape her psychological studies of meaning-making in suffering. Many sufferers sense at some point in their story that God is working in and through their hardships. This doesn't happen to everyone, and when it does, it may not happen as soon or as clearly as we hope. It also might not answer all our questions, and it doesn't justify misdeeds or injustices done to us. But it does put our suffering against the larger backdrop of God's presence and work.

Even if God's specific purposes are not clear to us, there are some general purposes for suffering that have been revealed to us in the Bible. These purposes don't seem to be just for specific people or specific time periods. Instead, they provide hints of the ways God uses our suffering to prepare all of us for closer relationship with him.

WHAT IS GOD UP TO? GENERAL PURPOSES FOR SUFFERING

Let's return to Romans 8:28, a verse commonly misused in the context of suffering. This verse assures us that God will redeem our suffering, that "all things"—including, we assume, our suffering—can be turned for our good, for God's purposes. But this verse doesn't occur in isolation.

In the next verse, Paul explains what that "good" is and what those purposes are: to be "conformed to the image of his Son" (v. 29). And just a few verses before verse 28, we find the context in which God acts for our good: our adoption as beloved children of God (vv. 14-16). The ultimate destination is that we experience Jesus as our older brother and God as our Father (v. 29) so that ultimately nothing, absolutely nothing, will be able to separate us from God's love (vv. 35-39).

Scripture states a number of ways God redeems suffering to fulfill the purpose of making us more like Jesus. Suffering can help deepen our relationship with Jesus, help us grow, and help us do the things Jesus does. As you read through these, consider what God might be doing in your life.

Suffering draws us into deeper friendship with Jesus. What do you do when you connect with friends you haven't seen or spoken to for a long time? Old friends reminisce about experiences they had together in the past. "Remember that time when . . . ?" Shared experiences draw people together in friendship. This is especially true for dramatic or difficult experiences. Soldiers who have fought together, for example, often report a profound sense of enduring connection long after battles are over.

Similarly, personal pain and suffering, whether caused by persecution or as the result of other losses and difficulties, are an opportunity to know Christ better because we are going through something he experienced. The apostle Paul describes his losses as a means to know Jesus better:

> What is more, I consider everything a loss because of the surpassing worth of knowing Christ Jesus my Lord, for whose sake I have lost all things. I consider them garbage, that I may gain Christ. . . . I want to know Christ—yes, to know the power of his resurrection and participation in his sufferings, becoming like him in his death, and so, somehow, attaining to the resurrection from the dead. (Philippians 3:8-11)

Our present suffering helps us empathize with Jesus' suffering. For example, when Jason felt betrayed by a coworker, he understood Jesus' pain at being betrayed much better. Similarly, a mother who lost her teenage son in an automobile accident told us her grief helped her "to better know the heart of God" since "many times I've thought, 'He, too, knows the pain of losing a son.'"

One of our participants, Lilah, described closeness with Jesus this way: "He prayed that the cup would be taken from him. He didn't want to go through crucifixion. He didn't want to die that horrible death. And that was a powerful moment of realization, like, oh wait, not only did God allow me to avoid death, but he understands intimately what it feels like to be scared of death. . . . Of course Jesus understands. He was literally praying to not have to go through this thing because he was so scared of it. And that was a powerful connection moment for me with my faith, realizing Jesus understands exactly how I feel." Many attest to similar experiences: even in their awful suffering they somehow feel greater intimacy with God rather than divine distance.

Here we are reminded that Christians navigating suffering are not left in a classroom debating an abstract conception of a deity, but we are those who look into the eyes of Christ as he bleeds and weeps on the cross. Jesus shapes our conception of God, and then how we imagine ourselves relating to God. Our God is not indifferent or unconcerned but has entered in, knows the human dilemma of pain and suffering, and meets us where we are.

Corrie Ten Boom was a Dutch woman who, with her family, hid many Jews from the Nazis. When this was discovered, she and her sister Betsie were sent to a concentration camp. Corrie recalled how she and Betsie felt closer to Jesus when they had their clothes taken from them in the camp as they remembered how Jesus' clothes had been taken, too. Because our life is a participation in Jesus' life (Galatians 2:20), our suffering is also connected to his, and we have an opportunity to know him better through it. Our faith, therefore, offers practices that can assist us in drawing near to Jesus through our sufferings.

Suffering helps us become more like Jesus. As Romans 8 shows us, suffering can help us take on the characteristics of Jesus. Sadly, sin gets in the way of relating to God in intimacy, even after we have been justified and our sins forgiven, because sin causes us to be internally fragmented.[4] We are often ashamed of parts of ourselves. Fearing rejection, we don't dare show them to others or even God. We may even hide these shameful parts from ourselves! When we are fragmented in this way, we can't bring all of ourselves into relationship with God. These hidden parts become barriers to wholehearted closeness with God. Shame leads to isolation, not intimacy.

Fragmentation also takes the form of conflicted desires. Closeness requires wholehearted commitment to the desire of connection with another person. But we rarely find ourselves with wholehearted desire for intimacy with God. While we may desire this kind of closeness at one level, we may at the same time desire things that prevent it, such as illegitimate power or sinful pleasures. The apostle Paul describes this internal fragmentation when he says, "I do not do the good I want to do, but the evil I do not want to do—this I keep on doing" (Romans 7:19).

Even when our desires are not sinful, they may compete with God. For example, Liz desires to be closer to God, but she has also found that being productive meets some of her needs to feel she is a worthwhile person. Consequently, when spending dedicated time with God, she struggles with restlessness and distracting thoughts of how to make progress in her various projects. Being productive is good, but sometimes we make it more important than intimacy with God.

Instead of competing with the desire to know God more fully, our desires should align with and support the goal of knowing God. If the purpose of suffering is to lead us into deeper communion with God, then one of the ways it does this is to facilitate the integration of our souls around God. We become more like Jesus, who oriented his entire life around God's purposes. In this way our lives move from fragmentation to integration: We are on the path to becoming more whole.

When faced well, suffering provides the kinds of circumstances that help us cultivate certain character traits. The Bible connects suffering with the development of virtues such as obedience (Hebrews 5:8), empathy and compassion (Hebrews 2:18), perseverance (James 1:2-4), and hope (Romans 5:3-5). Romans 5:3-4 states, "We also glory in our sufferings, because we know that suffering produces perseverance; perseverance, character; and character, hope." In some cases it's difficult to imagine how we would develop certain virtues in the absence of difficulties. How would we develop perseverance if we didn't face obstacles? How would we develop patience if things didn't tempt us toward irritation? Suffering can also allow us to grow by turning us away from unhealthy patterns or choices and moving us toward new goals.

Suffering may also help us become more like Jesus by purifying our faith. James 1:2-3 describes the trials we experience as "testing." Suffering is like the process skilled metalworkers use to see if the metal they are working with is pure. Suffering reveals our inner character and brings to the surface our true nature. Kelly recalls times in his life when he imagined he was stronger or more faithful than turned out to be the case when difficult circumstances arose. He also recognizes times when he was encouraged and even surprised to discover that suffering revealed a depth he wasn't yet sure was there: Seeing this growth brought fresh encouragement and hope. Suffering can illuminate ways God has matured and deepened us beyond what we previously appreciated until it becomes clear during a painful trial.

Sometimes suffering reveals emotional wounds that have not been healed and are shaping our responses. Does my "heart" theology match my "head" theology? Is God just a set of ideas or someone with whom I interact? Do I discover uncomfortable aspects of myself when I go through hard times? Am I loyal to God only when things are easy and I have what I want? Do I trust that God is good and wants the best for me even when I don't experience my circumstances as good? When our suffering tests our faith, it makes room for God to grow and purify it, for us to see what we may have previously ignored. Suffering often challenges our ideas about God and ourselves and provides a fruitful place for self-examination. When we engage in our suffering with openness, God often uses it to move us into a more authentic and trusting relationship with him.

Suffering helps us do the things Jesus does. Suffering equips us to comfort others the way Jesus does. In 2 Corinthians 1:4-5, Paul writes, "[God] comforts us in all our troubles, so that we can comfort those in any trouble with the comfort we ourselves receive from God. For just as we share abundantly in the sufferings of Christ, so also our comfort abounds through Christ." God conforms us to Jesus through our suffering by preparing us to comfort others. When we go through specific types of suffering, we more fully understand the experiences of others who have faced the same challenges. Our eyes become wide open to pain and suffering. Our grieving ears grow more attuned to what is really happening around us. Through these experiences God produces greater empathy in us for others. This increased understanding enables us to comfort and console our fellow sufferers. When we do this, we enter a divine outpouring of comfort in which we taste the waters of God's comfort and then have the opportunity to pass on God's kindness and compassion to others who suffer.

When we comfort others with God's comfort, God is working in and through us. As a side benefit, tending to the needs of others gets our minds off ourselves, often providing temporary relief from pain. It puts us more deeply into solid friendship with those to whom we minister. It increases our ability to receive ministry in return. It improves our ability to communicate with everyone, whether by listening more deeply or speaking more clearly. Our sensitivity to pain can convert into a sensitivity to the world around us, giving us more opportunities for compassion and joy. In this way we draw closer to God, seeing the world more and more the way God sees it.

Suffering also prepares us to share the good news of the kingdom of God, just as Jesus did. What kind of story do you tell about your suffering? Does God show up? What role does he play? We can place our story of suffering within the larger story of what God is doing in the world. Suffering provides opportunities to tell others the good news about who God is and what he has done for us. Writing from prison to the Philippians, Paul clearly saw his suffering as an opportunity. He explains:

> What has happened to me has actually served to advance the gospel. As a result, it has become clear throughout the whole palace guard and to everyone else that I am in chains for Christ. And because of my chains, most of the brothers and sisters have become confident in the Lord and dare all the more to proclaim the gospel without fear. (Philippians 1:12-14)

When we tell our story about what God is doing in our lives, we open up an authentic opportunity to introduce unbelievers to the God they have not yet met. We can also encourage our sisters and brothers in the faith who may be going through their own difficulties, as they see how God has faithfully sustained and kept us.

Telling our stories doesn't mean downplaying our difficulties or pretending all is well when it really isn't. But it does mean telling others how God has showed up in our difficulties. Our sufferings can give us a certain kind of authority; we know what we are talking about! When others hear how God has sustained us in circumstances that could have crushed us, this brings glory to God. Whether at the end of tremendous difficulty or in the darkness of its middle, we can declare God's goodness: our God is present and he hears; he sustains and cares for us.

PURPOSE, MEANING-MAKING, AND BELIEFS ABOUT SUFFERING

God can redeem our suffering by using it to take us further along the path of becoming more like Jesus and to strengthen our relationship with God. Understanding that God has purposes for our suffering is important for our meaning-making. One important part of our global meaning system is how we think about suffering and its meaning. Seeing purpose in our suffering—an important part of situational meaning—prevents the hard things that come into our lives from shattering us and our sense of place in the world. How we conceptualize our suffering matters. And there has been some psychological research on how different ways of thinking about suffering leads to different outcomes, either positive or negative.

Generally, having more violations of your global meaning system results in more post-traumatic symptoms. But having benevolent views of God in the middle of suffering results in less severe symptoms. How you think about your suffering, and specifically the purposes you see in your suffering, makes a difference. One study found that benevolent views of suffering (for example, the views that God in his providence has control over suffering, that God suffers along with us, and that God uses our suffering to build our character) served a protective function in adult survivors of the 2016 Louisiana floods.[5]

In these last three chapters, we have focused on the road ahead. In terms of the meaning-making model, we have thus far concentrated on the actual meanings our faith provides to give context to our suffering. The following chapters will provide some meaning-making practices of our faith that help us internalize those meanings.

For now, spend time with God asking what God might choose to do with your suffering. Is God making a flowerpot out of a broken wheelbarrow? How can you cooperate with God's purposes by continuing to bring your suffering into relationship with God and doing your part in accomplishing those purposes? The Bible encourages us to look forward in hope to see what God will do. He has given us a glimpse (and only a glimpse, mind you) of the end of the story in the book of Revelation. Most suffering is an ending of some kind: the ending of life, health, security, employment, comfort, relationship. Our own good requires that problematic things end: our ingratitude, complacency, and selfishness. Sometimes even good things need to end—things that are temporary and part of the limited life we live before Jesus returns. The Bible encourages us to keep our eyes open for new beginnings. Suffering is not the end of our journey.

FOR REFLECTION OR DISCUSSION

1. Take some time to reflect on a specific experience of suffering in your life. Write down any ways you have seen God work through this experience to deepen your relationship with him, to help you grow in Christlikeness, or to prepare you to minister to others. If you struggle to identify any clear purposes, ask God to give you eyes to see his hand at work in your life.

2. Of the purposes for suffering mentioned in the chapter, are there any you had not considered with respect to your suffering? Using the passages from this chapter, spend some time learning about that purpose. How might seeing this purpose for your suffering be helpful? How can you collaborate with the Holy Spirit in working toward this purpose?
3. Reflect on the following passages using lectio divina: James 1:2-8, 12; Romans 5:1-5; 2 Corinthians 1:3-7.

FURTHER READING

Gerald Sittser, *A Grace Disguised: How the Soul Grows Through Loss* (Zondervan, 2004).

C. S. Lewis, *The Problem of Pain* (New York: MacMillan, 1940).

Joni Eareckson Tada and Steven Estes, *When God Weeps* (Zondervan, 2000).

PART TWO

MEANING-MAKING PRACTICES FOR THE JOURNEY

FIVE

IDENTIFYING WITH CHRIST'S SUFFERING

Christ suffered and died for our sake, right? And so I think that as any Christian goes through any suffering, it gives us more of a connection to what Christ did for us, even though it's not the same. I mean, what he went through was much worse than anything I went through. But I think to some extent it helps me understand just a tiny, tiny bit of what Christ did for me.

Kevin, cancer survivor

Jewish artist Marc Chagall painted *White Crucifixion* in 1938 as Europe was already burning. In the center, Christ hangs on the cross—but this is not the Christ of stained glass windows or Sunday school flannel boards. This Christ is unmistakably Jewish. A prayer shawl, not a loincloth, wraps his waist. Above his head, the inscription reads not in Latin but in Hebrew, Yiddish, and Russian. His face is serene, almost peaceful, while around him the world convulses in violence.

To his right, a synagogue blazes. Flames leap from its roof as Torah scrolls scatter like wounded birds. Below, Jewish villagers flee with whatever they can carry—a mother clutches her child, an old man stumbles with his walking stick, families abandon their homes with bundles slung over their shoulders. A boat overflows with refugees. Revolutionary figures brandish red flags. Everything is motion, panic, displacement.

Still, the viewer is drawn not to the chaos surrounding Jesus but to Jesus himself. A great column of divine light streams down from heaven, illuminating Christ's figure and radiating outward. The face of Jesus is peaceful while all around him is turmoil. Chagall painted this as Hitler's persecution of the Jews was escalating, when the world seemed to be tearing apart at the seams. Yet he placed Jesus—the Jewish Jesus—right in the center of his people's agony. While the subject matter of the painting is grim, it's also full of hope—a hope stemming from Jesus' presence in the midst of the suffering.

Jesus, who is none other than God himself with us, anchors our hope amid trials. As the "suffering servant" and "man of sorrows" (Isaiah 53), Jesus took upon himself our suffering. The prophet Isaiah, who applied these titles to the coming Messiah many centuries before he was born, goes on to say, "Surely he took up our pain and bore our suffering" and delivers the news that "by his wounds we are healed" (Isaiah 53:4-5). The apostle Peter echoes these remarks when he concludes, "by [Jesus'] wounds you have been healed" (1 Peter 2:24). Because Jesus took our humanity upon himself, uniting himself with us, in him we also have hope of restoration and healing.

Sometimes we are so focused on how Jesus took our sins upon himself on the cross in order to reconcile us with God that we forget about sin's constant companion, suffering. Jesus came to destroy sin and also to heal us of the suffering sin inevitably brings. Some of this healing may happen in the present (for example, in reconciled relationships), and some of it will not come until much later (for example, when our bodies are fully renewed).

Knowing that Jesus took our suffering upon himself and is with us now in our own suffering can be immensely comforting. As Shawn, one of our participants, said about his cancer, "When I struggle, I'm able to go to him and say, 'Thank you, Lord, that you walked before me, and you know what I'm going through.' When we have struggles, there's such a comfort to know that he knows firsthand, and I can run to him. I don't run to someone who's never experienced what I'm talking about. I run to someone who's been there firsthand."

But what if the connection between Jesus and our suffering goes beyond that? What if it's not only true that Jesus can understand us better because he suffered, but also that we can understand Jesus better because we have suffered? What if one of the most important purposes of our suffering is to draw us closer to Jesus?

The way we appraise our suffering, the meaning we attribute to it, the way we wrap our brains around it, makes a big difference. It influences how we feel and it shapes what we do in response to our suffering. As one person who has dealt with profound tragedy explained to us, "The devastation still comes, the pain is still felt (since suffering doesn't hurt less as a believer), but knowing that we are participating in the fellowship of Christ's suffering brings a level of comfort and peace that nothing else in this world can offer—and a closeness to Christ that brings purpose to that pain." But how do we get to this point? Infusing our suffering with meaning, knowing that God is using our suffering to further God's purposes, helps to provide hope. And the biggest purpose of all is to help us find our way past all our limitations and barriers to experiencing more deeply our relationship with our holy and loving God.

And this brings us to the practice we are recommending in this chapter: identifying with Christ in his suffering. By "identifying with Christ" we mean contemplating him and what he went through, seeing that part of the humanity you have in common with him in the experience of suffering. We mean looking at what he does with his suffering, especially in his conversation with the Father. We mean asking how you might be transformed by following a pattern similar to his, not just because he sets a moral example for us but because he embodies God's solidarity with us even in our pain and suffering.

WHAT DOES IT MEAN TO IDENTIFY WITH CHRIST IN HIS SUFFERING?

Again and again in his writings, the apostle Paul hints at his experience of day-to-day contact with Christ's death and resurrection (Galatians 6:14; Galatians 2:19; Romans 6:6-7). He explains that our crucifixion with Christ helps us grow in the freedom from sin Christ's death accomplished for us. For example, Romans 6:6-7 says, "For we know that our old self was crucified with him so that the body ruled by sin might be done away with, that we should no longer be slaves to sin—because anyone who has died has been set free from sin." Yes, Christ's death and resurrection have accomplished the forgiveness of my sins, but this passage focuses elsewhere. It shows us that the crucifixion has not only destroyed the power of sin over me; it has changed the dynamics of my everyday life in which I encounter challenges and endure suffering. I am no longer a slave to sin. Christ's death and resurrection have transformed me and continue to transform me into increasing Christlikeness as I learn to live in this freedom from sin.

And this is where suffering comes in. Paul sees his own suffering as a form of death or dying related to Christ's death.[1] In Philippians 3:10-11, he writes, "I want to know Christ—yes, to know the power of his resurrection and participation in his sufferings, becoming like him in his death, and so, somehow, attaining to the resurrection from the dead." When Paul wrote these words he had already experienced the power of Christ's death and resurrection in the forgiveness of his sins. Yet in these verses he is speaking of something he wants to experience in the future. What is it that he wants to keep experiencing? What is the power of the resurrection and the fellowship of sharing in Christ's sufferings? What does it mean to become "like Christ in his death" (v. 10) and "attaining to the resurrection from the dead" (v. 11)?

In God's redemptive mercy for a broken world, moments of suffering provide significant occasions for connection with Christ's death and resurrection. Counterintuitively, God often takes the ugliness of suffering and makes it an opportunity. And, fortunately or unfortunately, depending on how you think about it, we have many of these moments of suffering in our daily lives. Luke, one of our participants, reflected on his time in treatment and said, "My message is until we've experienced the pain and suffering of Jesus, we do not have a full resurrection. . . . He experienced a lot more suffering than we'll ever experience in carrying our sins with him to the cross. . . . We experience that resurrection a little bit in this life. I think I feel like I've been resurrected, okay?" Philippians 3 and other passages like it suggest three interconnected ways we can "know Christ" in his suffering and resurrection, which we might also consider to be three pathways for transformation.

Identification as partnering with the Holy Spirit. First, Philippians 3 speaks of the power of God that accomplished Christ's resurrection and transforms our lives. Often this power is linked in the New Testament to the indwelling of the Holy Spirit. When we contemplate the connection of our suffering to Christ's suffering, we are partnering with the Holy Spirit as he transforms our lives. As we meditate on this connection, it changes our perspective on our suffering in ways that employ the Spirit's power in our lives.[2] We can see our suffering not just as an unwanted pain but as an opportunity to know Christ better, which keeps us from being consumed by the many things we cannot change. It refocuses our mind on the hope and healing we have in Jesus. This in turn brings us into conversation with our Lord and into active participation with the Holy Spirit in shaping a Jesus-oriented life. This is a means by which God not only changes us but also uses us to love others around us. We can think of our endurance of suffering as a joint project between us and the Holy Spirit. How does the Spirit want to use our suffering to point us to Jesus?

Identification as following in Christ's steps. A second way we can understand and express our connection with Christ's suffering is to contemplate how Jesus responded to suffering and follow his example. 1 Peter 2:21 says, "Christ suffered for you, leaving you an example, that you should follow in his steps." This passage views Jesus' suffering not simply as a means of salvation for us but also as a pattern to guide our lives. As a seventy-seven-year-old woman who lived a hard life on the Mexican-American border spoke of her suffering, she highlighted the courage it gave her to contemplate Jesus' suffering: "If [Jesus] suffered, and [he] could do anything, why couldn't we?"[3]

How did Jesus suffer?[4] First, instead of allowing his suffering to distance him from the Father, Jesus brought his suffering to God. Hebrews 5:7 says, "During the days of Jesus' life on earth, he offered up prayers and petitions with fervent cries and tears to the one who could save him from death, and he was heard because of his reverent submission." People who suffer sometimes turn away from God in anger or disappointment. Jesus' example encourages us instead to turn to God with our suffering, and to do so in a way that expresses fully what we are feeling.

Paloma is a young woman who had been in a relationship where she experienced abuse. When interviewed, she showed steadfastness in bringing her suffering to God: "I remember just crying out to God in pain and agony and needing him. And I used to read through the Psalms, which are all about anguish and crying out to God. . . . I don't think I could put [those feelings] into words myself, apart from crying out, 'Just help me and heal me and make me whole, and help me to be myself again and to be confident and trust people.' So going through those psalms really, really helped."[5] We follow Jesus' approach to suffering when we bring all of it in prayer before the Father.

Second, in response to suffering Jesus did not waver from following the Father, who had allowed this suffering into his life. Instead of responding sinfully by ignoring the Father and looking for relief elsewhere, he continued to listen to the Father by the mediation of the Holy Spirit (see, for example, Luke 4:1-17). Nor did he retreat from kindness, even toward those who abused him: "When they hurled their insults at him, he did not retaliate; when he suffered, he made no threats" (1 Peter 2:23). The biblical writers tell us Jesus grew in character through his experiences, learning obedience and gaining empathy and compassion for us (Hebrews 2:9-18; 5:7-10). When we are suffering, we often respond in sinful ways by retaliating or treating those around us poorly. Jesus did not do this. Instead he demonstrated virtue in his response to suffering. When bad things happen to us, we need to pause and consider wise and loving responses. Usually this will be difficult and require us to practice. The work of the Holy Spirit through formative practices can shape us into those who obey God even in difficult circumstances. We might, for example, practice responding with prayer when others belittle us. Similarly, we should seek positive outlets for alleviating physical or mental distress, such as savoring simple pleasures and connecting with loved ones.

Third, Jesus practiced what we might call "perspective-taking"—that is, because he knew whose Son he was, what he was doing, where he was going, and what his suffering would accomplish, he had a perspective that allowed him to see beyond the immediate sufferings to a goal that eclipsed them. There is a key link between his purpose and his attitude when it came to his suffering: "For the joy set before him [Jesus] endured the cross, scorning its shame, and sat down at the right hand of the throne of God" (Hebrews 12:2). He endured his suffering in light of the glory that was to come (Luke 24:26; 1 Peter 1:11). His suffering was horrendous and deeply appalling, yet somehow he could experience not just the ache of lament (Mark 15:34; Psalm 22:1) but also the sustaining power of purpose and life-giving joy (Hebrews 12:2).

In Romans 8:18, Paul encourages us to do the same kind of perspective-taking, writing, "I consider that our present sufferings are not worth comparing with the glory that will be revealed in us," and elsewhere, "Our light and momentary troubles are achieving for us an eternal glory that far outweighs them all" (2 Corinthians 4:17). This strategy can help us transform our experiences so that they have new meaning: Following Jesus' example, we interpret our suffering in light of the glory that is to come (conformity to Christ) and mindful of how the suffering might help us achieve this end. We gain perspective by noticing what God is doing. How has God been kind to us through our difficulty? Trusted friends and family can provide a listening ear to put our situations into bigger contexts of our lives, the lives of our families and friends, and God's people throughout history. How will we evaluate our challenges five years from now? Fifteen years from now? Five hundred years from now?

Identification as intimacy. Contemplating the presence of Christ in our sufferings and considering our sufferings to be a participation in his can move us into greater intimacy with Christ. The phrase "fellowship of his sufferings" in Philippians 3:10 (KJV) suggests a closeness to Christ that comes from the shared experience of suffering. Romans 8, which speaks at length of suffering, concludes that in suffering believers are "more than conquerors through him who loved us" (Romans 8:37). This verse is surrounded by exuberant depictions of the love of Christ for us. Just as Christ's suffering demonstrated God's love for us, so our suffering can be, in the words of theologian Michael Gorman, "a continuation of the narrative of divine love."[6] Suffering can move us more deeply into experiencing Christ's love as we participate in the fellowship of his suffering. Our friendship with Jesus grows by connecting our experiences to his. Consider the ways you have suffered. In what ways did Jesus experience this or something like it? What would it have been like for Jesus to experience that? How is your experience like his? These shared experiences draw us closer together.

At its root, our suffering is caused by the fallenness of the world. This very fallenness was what Christ came to confront. Christ's suffering was central to his mission and identity. When we align our suffering with Christ's, we recognize the necessary conflict between Christ's followers and the world, which Jesus describes in John 15:18-25. These verses remind us that the world hates us because it hates Christ. We often interpret this passage as referring to persecution by unbelievers, but it also refers to the world as a fallen cosmos dominated by the prince of the power of the air. In John 16:33, Jesus concludes by saying, "I have told you these things, so that in me you may have peace. In this world you will have trouble. But take heart! I have overcome the world." We participate in the sufferings of Christ because the only life we have is his life in us, and that life is in fundamental conflict with the fallen world. Thus, when we use our suffering as an opportunity to share in the suffering of Christ, our consciousness of that shared experience facilitates relational intimacy.[7] We simply know Christ better.

At this point you may be asking yourself, *If identifying with Christ's suffering is such a foundational Christian practice, why have I never heard of it?* Over the centuries we have neglected many important resources that our faith gives us for suffering well. But there are pockets of Christianity that have maintained these resources. We get glimpses of this in the stories of our brothers and sisters captured in psychological research.

THE PSYCHOLOGICAL RESEARCH

Until our team began to study how identifying with Christ's suffering made a difference in people's lives, this topic had never been studied—at least, not on purpose. Sometimes, when psychologists interviewed people who had gone through tough times, they unexpectedly stumbled on this connection with Christ's suffering. One study of older Mexican Americans who live along the Texas-Mexico border found that participants saw suffering as a necessary part of life because Jesus suffered when he was crucified.[8] When they suffered, they felt they were following in Jesus' footsteps by taking on pain and suffering as he did and that this shared experience helped them feel a closer bond to him. One seventy-two-year-old woman, in describing her response to her cancer diagnosis, said, "I believe that we have to suffer in order to also learn and give more value to [Jesus'] suffering. Because when I [was] going through suffering . . . all I said was, 'God, I give it to you. It was nothing compared to what you suffered.'"

In another qualitative study, several women with histories of trauma, including sexual abuse and domestic violence, saw their suffering as a way of connecting with Christ in his suffering.[9] One woman eloquently stated, "There's a deeper level of meaning as to what suffering's all about. Like it's a real honor to suffer, in a way it's like being like our Christ." Another spoke of Jesus' experience on the cross and said, "I guess to know that Jesus went through that process . . . I know that I'm not the only one that goes through the process." They spoke of experiencing God more deeply as a result of their trauma.

In yet another study, Chinese Christians who had been persecuted for their faith, enduring experiences such as imprisonment and a labor camp, also saw their suffering as a way of connecting with Christ's suffering.[10] Nearly half the participants in this study described feeling encouraged by intimate personal connections with the passions of Christ, including events both before and during his crucifixion. In line with what the previous studies showed, they reported greater closeness to God. One man said, "Through suffering we experience God. Through suffering we see God's glory."

In our own research, we developed a measure of identification with Christ in his suffering and have used it to explore how this way of approaching suffering relates to several outcomes.[11] In a large online sample of Christians who reported they had gone through a difficult life event in the past six months, we found that people who identified with Christ in their suffering also described increased satisfaction with life and positive emotions, as well as decreased negative emotions. The relationship was particularly strong with satisfaction with life. In other words, even when people continue to experience some of the hard feelings associated with difficult life events, the profound purpose found in connecting their suffering with Jesus' suffering brought the kind of satisfaction associated with having a life filled with meaning. Similarly, in another study we found that identifying with Christ's suffering helped buffer the distress that results from negative life events.[12] Generally, there is a strong relationship between the severity of the difficult life event and levels of depression and anxiety. The more severe the event, the greater the depression and anxiety. But identifying one's suffering with Christ's suffering weakened this relationship, indicating that some people did not experience as much distress as expected.

Together, these studies show that identifying or connecting with Christ's suffering can be helpful to Christians who are suffering. It brings an important and transcendent purpose to the suffering, alleviating distress and increasing a sense that life is meaningful. But most importantly, this way of conceptualizing suffering is connected to a deeper and more intimate relationship with God in Christ.

NUTS AND BOLTS: HOW TO PRACTICE IDENTIFYING WITH CHRIST

In its most basic form, identifying with Christ's suffering is very straightforward. It simply means thinking of your suffering related to Christ's suffering. Sometimes they are connected in specific ways. If you have been betrayed, Jesus was betrayed too. If you suffer physical pain, Jesus knew what it was like to endure excruciating pain. If you have been abandoned by friends and family to face your suffering alone, Jesus knows what that is like too. If you have suffered homelessness, Jesus has too. If you don't know where your next meal is coming from, Jesus also experienced hunger. Have you lost a parent or a loved one? Jesus did too. Are you a refugee? Jesus was too. You might want to take some time to just sit with the sense that Jesus understands what you're going through and is with you.

But don't stop there. See if you can take your inner focus off your own suffering and focus on Jesus' suffering. What was his experience of betrayal, of physical pain, of abandonment like? Stay with Jesus in those places.

Perhaps the most foundational practice for identifying with Christ's suffering was established by Jesus himself. In the Gospel of John, Jesus told his followers that he was the bread of life and that he would give his own body for the life of the world (John 6:35, 51). Before his death, he again used bread as a metaphor for his suffering, saying, "This is my body, broken for you" (1 Corinthians 11:24 MSG). He went on to instruct his followers to remember his broken body, his suffering, whenever they met together. Starting with this meal, Christians have regularly followed Jesus' instructions in a variety of ways, from literal breaking of a loaf that is passed around the congregation, to a ritualized eating of a wafer that is dispensed by a priest.

There are layers of meanings involved in the practice of remembering Christ's broken body, but they all begin with remembering and continue with eating. In a metaphorical sense, we identify with Christ's suffering as this symbol of his suffering is ingested and becomes part of our own bodies. This regular part of the life of the church is an opportunity to practice identifying with Christ's suffering. As we physically take in the bread that nourishes our bodies, we spiritually take in what he went through to accomplish our salvation. As we physically digest the bread, we spiritually internalize and identify with Christ's suffering.

In addition to this foundational and central practice of remembering Christ's suffering through the bread and wine practiced regularly by Christians around the world, other practices to support identification with Christ have been developed throughout the ages. In the 1500s, Ignatius of Loyola recommended a form of prayer that draws on our imaginations. He was convinced that God can work within our imaginations as much as through our thoughts and memories. To practice Ignatian prayer, imagine scenes from the Gospels that depict Jesus' suffering. Visualize one of these scenes as if you were seeing a movie, paying attention to the sights, sounds, tastes, smells, and feelings. After you have a sense for what the event was like, put yourself in the scene. Where does your imagination place you? What is the Holy Spirit telling you through this experience? What gut or physical reactions do you have? What do you learn about Jesus?

Sometimes our imaginations can be aided by reflecting on art portraying Jesus' suffering that has been gifted to us by our brothers and sisters in Christ who have used their God-given talents for God's glory. A centuries-old Christian practice called the stations of the cross involves systematically moving through all the events of the last days of Christ's life, pausing before pictures of each event to meditate on Christ's suffering. Many versions of the stations of the cross are available online or in more liturgically oriented churches.

Poetry is another gift that can aid us in this task of identifying with Christ's suffering. As with visual images, poetry helps us experience what it is portraying. For example, Malcolm Guite has written a series of poems illustrating the stations of the cross. Listen to how he describes Jesus' death on the cross. Imagine yourself there with him:

> The dark nails pierce him and the sky turns black,
> We watch him as he labours to draw breath.
> He takes our breath away to give it back,
> Return it to its birth through his slow death.
> We hear him struggle, breathing through the pain,
> Who once breathed out his spirit on the deep,
> Who formed us when he mixed the dust with rain
> And drew us into consciousness from sleep.

His Spirit and his life he breathes in all,
Mantles his world in his one atmosphere,
And now he comes to breathe beneath the pall
Of our pollutions, draw our injured air
To cleanse it and renew. His final breath
Breathes and bears us through the gates of death.[13]

A word of warning. Sometimes Christians, in a misguided attempt to identify with Christ's sufferings, have intentionally inflicted harm on themselves. The history of Christianity tells of people whipping themselves, crawling on rough surfaces for miles during pilgrimages, and even having themselves nailed to crosses in order to physically participate in Christ's suffering. These practices miss the point of New Testament teachings on identifying with Christ's suffering. We may face suffering in order to obey Christ's commands, and certainly ordinary life brings with it substantial suffering. But causing our own suffering is a rejection of the life Christ died to give us. While God can redeem our suffering as we use our suffering to draw closer to the suffering Christ, we must never make the mistake of seeing suffering as a good in and of itself.

Strange as it may sound, we have become convinced that suffering that comes our way is an opportunity. While it's comforting that Christ became a human and consequently understands our suffering, perhaps it's even more important that through suffering we can somehow understand Christ's suffering and personally draw closer to him. When we think of our suffering in this way, we partner with the Holy Spirit in doing God's work in our life. We think of how Christ suffered and try to understand suffering the way he did. As our view of the world aligns more and more closely with Christ's, we are able to know him more intimately. We don't experience the benefits of the cross in spite of suffering; we experience the benefits of the cross through suffering, as suffering is used to transform us.

FOR REFLECTION OR DISCUSSION

1. Practice Ignatian contemplation as a means to identify with Christ. Choose a Gospel passage that depicts a moment of Christ's suffering (for example, the rejection of the religious leaders, the agony in the garden, the crucifixion). Spend time prayerfully imagining yourself in the scene, using all your senses. What do you see, hear, feel, and experience? How does this encounter with Christ's suffering affect you? Journal about your reflections.
2. Draw closer to Christ's suffering through the use of art. Choose a poem or image of Christ's suffering that speaks to you. Examples include Malcolm Guite's stations of the cross poems or paintings like *Christ Crucified* by Diego Velázquez or the *Isenheim Altarpiece* by Matthias Grünewald. Each work of art is an incarnation of the events of the crucifixion into a particular time and place. For example, Grünewald's Christ has skin lesions covering his body because the piece hung in a monastery hospital for those suffering from skin diseases. Pay attention to the details, colors, and symbols in the piece, and consider how these elements evoke emotions or insights related to Christ's suffering and your own experiences. Reflect on questions such as:
   - What aspects of Christ's suffering does this artwork highlight?
   - How does the artist's unique perspective contribute to your understanding of Christ's suffering?

- In what ways do you see your own story reflected in this depiction?
- What emotions or thoughts arise as you sit with this artwork, and how might God be speaking to you through these responses?
- Journal about your reflections or respond to the artwork through your own creative expression.

3. Reflect on these passages using lectio divina: Isaiah 53:3-5; Philippians 3:10-11; Hebrews 4:14-16.

FURTHER READING

John Stott, *The Cross of Christ* (InterVarsity Press, 2006).
Alister McGrath, *Knowing Christ* (WaterBrook, 2002).
Thomas à Kempis, *The Imitation of Christ,* c. 1418-1427.

SIX

LAMENT

It was almost like an existential crisis, I would say, because this worldview that I had was really turned on its head. . . . I never gave myself permission to be honest with God. I think for a long time I really felt like I needed to put up a face for him because I wanted to give him what he wanted. But I had a wrong idea of what he wanted. He wants honesty from us. And I think going through the psalms of lament definitely woke me up to this idea [that] God doesn't just want us when we're happy. You know, he wants us when we [simply] are.

Laura, recovering from loss of job

As one might expect, Liz's year of treatment for breast cancer was grueling. She had several surgeries and a lot of physical pain, and during her months of chemotherapy, the antinausea drugs kept her awake for days at a time, so she was often exhausted. Medical insurance and scheduling issues added more stress. And for a special touch of gloom, the metallic taste in her mouth made it impossible to enjoy one of her greatest pleasures in life: coffee! But worse than the physical discomfort and the hassles were the recurring fears that the cancer would progress and leave her children without a mother and her husband without a wife. During those difficult months, it was a relief for her to be able to express her fears candidly to her husband and a close friend. They never seemed to mind hearing the same things again and again, even when the fears sounded crazy to Liz herself! And Liz found great comfort in the hour or so every morning when she spent time with God, crying out, asking for mercy, or simply sitting with God, finding comfort and some rest despite her insomnia.

It wasn't until after treatment had ended that Liz ran across the concept of biblical lament. Here was a method, found throughout the Psalms, for pouring out her troubles to God and finding strength in him.

THE PRACTICE OF LAMENT

Biblical lament provides a powerful form of prayer that embeds us firmly in fellowship with God and strengthens our position for understanding and dealing with suffering. It's a structured way of connecting with God in prayer (or song) as a response to our suffering, found extensively in the Psalms and displayed throughout the New Testament.

As a practicing Jew, Jesus would have participated in the communal praying and singing of the Psalms, including the psalms of lament. This formed the backdrop for his own personal practice of lament. Jesus consistently brought his suffering to his Father: Hebrews 5:7 says, "During the days of Jesus' life on earth, he offered up prayers and petitions with fervent cries and tears to the one who could save him from death, and he was heard because of his reverent submission."

When Jesus faced the suffering of others, as when Lazarus died, he lamented (John 11:28-44). When he faced his upcoming death in the garden of Gethsemane, he lamented. On the cross he cried out, "My God, my God, why have you forsaken me?" (Matthew 27:46), quoting the beginning of Psalm 22, a psalm of lament. Shortly afterward, Jesus prayed yet another psalm of lament before dying, Psalm 31:5, crying out, "Father, into your hands I commit my spirit." We can use the same psalms that Jesus used to voice our lament at the pain of the world.

Unfortunately, the practice of lament has almost disappeared from contemporary Christian culture in America. There are signs of renewed interest, but the regular practice of lament remains far from many of our congregations. The psalms we most often read and sing in our places of worship are those that offer praise and thanksgiving to God. Those that voice distress are under-represented in public worship: a recent study of contemporary hymnals concluded that only about 4 percent of hymns reflect the kind of lament modeled in the Psalms,[1] in stark contrast to the 40 percent of psalms in the hymnal of Israel that are laments. Along similar lines, drawing data from CCLI's "Top 100 Worship Songs," others have argued that this neglect of lament, when tied together with a proclivity toward sentimentality, causes us to ignore songs focused on injustice and thus makes us ill-prepared for when our communities suffer misfortune or harm.[2] At least in America, we tend to focus on the positive and downplay the negative. But that is not always a helpful approach.

From a psychological perspective, suffering can destroy our sense of meaning and leave us reeling in a world that no longer makes sense. Lament promotes the creation of new meaning by providing a narrative arc for the meaning-making story to emerge.

The psalms of lament move us from the threat of disruption and confusion to the creation of new meaning, from the chaos of a shattered worldview to the order of a stronger worldview, from suffering to worship. Lament is prayer that speaks to God about the pain and brokenness in our lives. It is both relational and directional. We connect with God while we move from a place of struggle to a place of surrender and trust. We shift from a focus on our self and our struggles to a focus on God. In this chapter, we will walk through the story and structure of lament. We'll be using Psalm 13 to illustrate each of the elements. It's worth slowly reading through before we break it down:

How long, Lord? Will you forget me forever?
  How long will you hide your face from me?
How long must I wrestle with my thoughts
  and day after day have sorrow in my heart?
  How long will my enemy triumph over me?

Look on me and answer, Lord my God.
  Give light to my eyes, or I will sleep in death,
and my enemy will say, "I have overcome him,"
  and my foes will rejoice when I fall.

But I trust in your unfailing love;
  my heart rejoices in your salvation.
I will sing the Lord's praise,
  for he has been good to me.

STRUCTURE OF A LAMENT

When you watch a movie or read a book, you can intuitively sense if it is a good story. This is because good stories have structures that take you from the beginning to the end. The psalms of lament also have a structure.

Calling out to God. The psalms of lament typically begin by crying out to God. Psalm 13, for example, starts, "How long, LORD?" We need to know it's okay to approach God and speak from our hearts. The lament psalms connect us in our suffering with God. Beyond merely venting our frustrations or grumbling and complaining, in lament we bring our experiences, including our suffering, to God. This is part of learning to be open with God in prayer.[3]

We have all been in relationships where we didn't really matter to the other person, perhaps with a boss or a professor. The other person called all the shots in the relationship. We simply responded. There was no room for our own concerns, needs, or preferences—best to keep all of that to oneself. We had no confidence that presenting our desires would produce a useful result. This kind of relationship lacks intimacy. In our closest relationships, perhaps with a spouse, friend, or family member, chances are that we initiate in the relationship to describe the important things happening in our lives and our responses to those events. When we do so, the other person probably (hopefully!) responds with understanding, or helps us figure out what comes next, or simply provides a listening ear. These are the people we want for friends.

God is very big and powerful, but he is not like the powerful people who are absorbed with their own concerns and goals without room for the needs of others. Instead, God invites us to be active in our fellowship with him, to call out to him in our triumphs and our fears—to take initiative in the relationship. He doesn't put us on hold while we hope for some acknowledgment that he has noticed us. "Draw near to God, and he will draw near to you" (James 4:8 ESV).

Of course, the psalms were all written long before Jesus was born. And further, Jesus' life, death, and resurrection radically changed the nature of our relationship with God. Now we can see in Jesus the evidence of God's love for us and the solution for the sin and suffering that had kept us from God. Whereas the psalmists looked forward to God's promised presence and deliverance in the Messiah, we see that God did what he promised in sending us Jesus. He is the Son of God, Immanuel—God with us (Matthew 1:23). And yet Jesus is also truly human, our elder brother (Romans 8:29; Hebrews 2:11), our compassionate and sympathetic high priest (Hebrews 4:14–5:10). Because of Jesus, when we call out to God, we can call him our Father. The Old Testament Jews had an image of God as a Father, but this was not a central part of how they thought of God. Jesus' emphatic and repeated use of *Abba* to refer to God—a term of intimacy—was adopted by Paul (Romans 8:15; Galatians 4:6). Because believers have the Spirit of Christ in them, Paul encouraged them to go before God in the certainty that God was their loving heavenly Father.

Complaining to God. The second component of lament invites us to wrestle with God regarding the cause of our suffering. For example, Psalm 13:1-2 says:

> Will you forget me forever?
> How long will you hide your face from me?
> How long must I wrestle with my thoughts
> and day after day have sorrow in my heart?
> How long will my enemy triumph over me?

Psalm 13 speaks specifically of enemies, but the psalms of lament record complaints about a wide variety of things: physical suffering, disappointments in life, depression, and people who have hurt us. The complaint sometimes focuses on God himself, which is startling to our church culture, even unnerving. But it is also honest. The Psalms repeatedly document deep questions like "God, where are you?" and "God, if you love me, then why?" In Psalm 13, the psalmist accuses God of hiding from him! Nothing is off-limits in honestly expressing our suffering to God. Doubts about God, anger at God, hatred of our enemies—God is open to hearing whatever is in our hearts.

Again, this is remarkable! In our other relationships, our honesty is often restrained by other powerful factors, such as concern for others' well-being or fear of their reaction. God alone is big enough and good enough to hear what is truly in our hearts. He does not require us to first become clean, proper, or eloquent when we come to him—he just wants us to come.

Often when taking Christians through the teaching and practice of lament, Kelly has found that believers respond with concern. Sometimes this idea of "complaining" can hit Christians badly, and they understandably worry that doing so might be wrong. When hearing about lament, again and again people ask, "Didn't God get upset with the Israelites for complaining?" This is a great question that takes us to the heart of the problem. When we voice our questions, hurts, and frustrations directly to God, he is quick to listen and he is compassionate in his response. Yet when we speak about God to others, belittling him or raising questions about his wisdom and character, then problems arise. Simply put, "complaining" is not completely ruled out, but we are invited to complain personally and honestly to our Sovereign Lord himself, rather than to gripe about God to others. Counterintuitively, complaining to God can be an authentic expression of faith, while complaining about God to others usually indicates a painful example of disbelief and an antagonistic orientation toward God.

Several of our participants followed the psalmists in wrestling with God in prayer. Sarai normalized this, saying "I never blamed God, but I do remember asking God why. And I think that's normal. I think it's okay to ask why. And I think God's big enough that he can handle our questions. I don't think God is offended by our questions. . . . Everybody has a moment of doubt and disbelief . . . but it's what you do with that, you know?"

Glen did blame God! He said, "I remember kinda blaming God at some point. I was so angry. I'm thinking, 'Where are you in this, God? You're a fixer, right? You fix things. And this isn't good. This isn't good.' And I didn't feel him. I felt abandoned . . . but I think what happens is grief can cloud our vision. And I was so overwhelmed with grief I couldn't see God anywhere. I couldn't feel him anywhere. In hindsight, I realized he was there all along."

Psychological research suggests that growth requires us to process suffering cognitively and emotionally, the way it is done in lament.[4] This takes time and deliberation. Thoughtlessly complaining about God dishonors him and erodes our ability to handle the situation before us. Lamenting to God not only honors the Lord; it reaffirms our agency by acknowledging its true nature—that is, that our action rests on our dependence on God. In fact, some studies suggest that the amount of growth we experience as a result of our suffering is directly related to the amount of intentional time we spend wrestling with the suffering—in other words, being involved in the meaning-making process.[5] We have heard, from people who suffered great losses, that they often felt like Christians and church settings pushed them to rush through grief. Ongoing wrestling can feel counterintuitive to people who don't understand the depths of suffering, but such struggle is part of the healing. And while this wrestling can and should happen with others, it must also centrally happen with God himself.

Bringing our requests to God. While it is not helpful to suppress thinking about our suffering, neither is it helpful to get stuck in it. The third element of lament, the request, acknowledges God as the one who can do something about our suffering. Psalm 13:3 implores, "Look on me and answer, LORD my God. Give light to my eyes." The psalmist knows what he wants and he asks God for it: he wants to know that God sees him and responds to him!

When we bring our requests to God, we acknowledge that God has the power to change our circumstances and has our best interests at heart. This acknowledgment reminds us of God's ability and his love, so it brings us hope. And this is the hope we need to regain our sense of meaning and balance. Study after study in the psychological literature shows that hope is central to feeling that life has meaning and to human flourishing.[6] We need hope in our darkness.

Generic hope is a rather vague psychological construct, expressing a sense of optimism about the future. But Christian hope connects us specifically with the God who eventually makes everything whole, including ourselves. Our hope has a particular direction, centered on God and his renewal of creation. Paul describes this in 2 Corinthians 4:17-18, writing, "Our light and momentary troubles are achieving for us an eternal glory that far outweighs them all. So we fix our eyes not on what is seen, but on what is unseen, since what is seen is temporary, but what is unseen is eternal."

The particular content of Christian hope does not dismiss our current suffering in the light of glory to come. That would only silence sufferers by distracting them from their current circumstances. Instead, our hope reminds us that we live in a transitional age and that our current suffering, though real, is temporary. Christ has defeated suffering and death, but we are still living in anticipation of the end of the story. The content of our future hope is eternal, but we still have cause to lament in our hope: we "groan as we wait," to use the language of Romans 8. Our suffering does not disappear, but we understand it in a different context. Our present suffering is not simply about us and the tragedies we can see; it is about our participation in Christ and the spiritual conflicts we don't see, about his victory and our part in it, which will eventually be shown to us. The presence of the God who saves his people and the perspective he gives make a huge difference in how we experience our suffering.

Remembering who God is. In the fourth element of lament, the psalmist seems to remind God of what God has done for the psalmist and for Israel. It may strike us as funny that the psalmist feels it's useful to remind God of what God has done, but this also serves to remind us of who God is. In this stage of the lament, the psalmist normally acknowledges God as God—that is, the psalmist puts us in touch with the true circumstances that confront us and not just the most painful ones.

This reminder has two aspects. First, we recall our position before the Almighty Holy One. God is God and we are not. God is the Creator and we are the creature. God is omniscient, omnipotent, and omnipresent. We are not. Suffering makes our limitations—our finitude, vulnerability, lack of control—very clear to us. But the presence of the Lord of the universe transforms our limitations into a specific need for him. This makes sense of the psychological research finding that the more overwhelming our circumstances and the more out of control we feel, the more potential for growth we experience. In the presence of God, our lack of control leads us to see his hand at work. Intimacy with God is not the intimacy of peers. It is more like a child's intimacy with a parent, blown up to cosmic proportions. Accordingly, lament reminds us of our position in relation to God.

Second, it also reminds us of the character of God. God has acted powerfully in the past, and we are reminded of God's "name"—that is, God is just and kind, loving and powerful. He is able and willing to act on behalf of the sufferer. As we bring our suffering to God, remembering his acts in the past reminds us of who God still is in the present. Our God's character never changes.

We are prone to forget the past. We get so fascinated by present difficulties that we have a hard time stepping back to see the larger context. This is why the Bible so often tells us to remember. The book of Deuteronomy is filled with God's instructions to the Israelites to "remember, remember, remember." They were instructed to set up piles of stones to remember important events. They were trained to set aside certain days of the week to remember. They were told to pass these memories on to their children as they sat at home, walked along the road, went to bed, and woke up each morning. They were told to remember the words of God's blessing (Deuteronomy 6:4-5) by wearing them on their hands and foreheads and by writing them on the door frames of their houses and gates. During times of sorrow, it is important to remember what God has done for us throughout our lives. Biblical lament helps us remember God's faithfulness.

Praising God. The last component, found in all but one or maybe two of the psalms of lament, is the expression of confidence in God. It completes the movement from suffering to praise and worship. The transition into this part of lament is often marked with the words *but* or *yet*. They signal that the psalmist has crossed a line, shifting the focus from the psalmist's pain to an acknowledgment of God's care. The transition can seem abrupt and even startling. Psalm 13 ends,

> But I trust in your unfailing love;
>   my heart rejoices in your salvation.
> I will sing the LORD's praise,
>   for he has been good to me. (Psalm 13:5-6)

Sometimes more lament will follow an outburst of praise, and the psalmist will move back and forth between the two, but in Psalm 13 it simply ends in praise.

Suffering itself does not necessarily lead to worship. We don't want to romanticize suffering nor imagine that simply going through it brings positive results. Many people become bitter and alienated from God. This is why the practice of lament is so vital. The Psalms do not specify what it is in the process of lament before God that leads believers back into praise, worship, and intimacy with God. Has God already acted? Perhaps. But it's also likely that a psychological shift happens here, some kind of internal and spiritual change, rather than a change in circumstances.

Based on our research interviewing many people who suffer, we believe that their surrender to God, an internal action of releasing the situation into his hands, enables a meaningful transition to praise. Even when God has not yet acted, the movement through the lament can lead us to this place of worship. Praying through the Psalms, calling out to God, pouring out our hearts and petitions to him, and reminding ourselves who God is—this movement reshapes our desires, affections, and outlook. For sufferers, lament and worship go together.

In our everyday walk with God, we may cultivate attitudes of humility, praise, and thanksgiving. But everyday circumstances do not usually strip from us our illusions of autonomy, self-determination, and control. Suffering and disaster drop us into utter helplessness, removing those illusions. They open our eyes to the reality that we are finite, created for fellowship with and dependence on a loving, all-powerful, all-knowing God. The appearance that we could control things was always a mirage. Facing the true nature of our place in the world reminds us of its Creator-creature structure, the presence of our loving heavenly Father, and the wisdom of relying on him.

Praise completes the story of lament—and, yes, lament itself is a story within a bigger story. It moves from calling out to God through our complaints and requests to a place of surrender, reliance, and care. Thus, lament becomes life-giving worship—the appropriate and practical response to a loving God who holds our lives in his hands. Beloved pastor Eugene Peterson wrote that this is the lesson of the Psalms, "that all true prayer pursued far enough will become praise. . . . It does not always get there quickly. It does not always get there easily . . . but the end is always praise."[7]

FINAL THOUGHTS ABOUT LAMENT

Psychological distress is caused by a gap between our understanding of our suffering and our larger views about the world and our place in it. The psalms of lament help us to bridge this gap. When our worldview is weak, lacking in nuance, or out of touch with the world, lament helps us rebuild it by reminding us of the foundational reality of a loving God and our fellowship with him as creatures and intimate dialogue partners. Lament puts our suffering into the larger context of God's redemptive activity. God is in control of this world that we find so uncontrollable. We find relief when we derive the meaning of our suffering from its place in the tapestry of God's faithfulness, celebrated in the Psalms.

The psalms of lament are a rich resource for those who suffer and for those who come alongside them. Using the Psalms to practice lament opens our spirit to God's presence and activity, teaching us how to see him and rest in his care even with the pain. They show us paths for bringing our difficulties before God. Lament does not function as a kind of magical formula, a collection of "right words" that instantly change our experience. As with all spiritual disciplines, we practice lament as a way of engaging with the Holy Spirit in our transformation. This is not a one-time event but a regular habit that gives structure to our slow molding into Christ's image.

Sometimes we are told, "Just trust God. Just have faith," as if these were easy options that required no more than a decision. They are not. Faith does, of course, require daily decisions of repeatedly turning to God. Practicing lament does not automatically produce anything, because God is not a mechanism and neither are we. Drawing on Augustine's insights, theologian

Todd Billings writes, "The Psalms are given to us as a divine pedagogy for our affections—God's way of reshaping our desires and perceptions so that they learn to lament in the right things and take joy in the right things."[8] When we come before God in lament, we are submitting to God in confidence that he will teach us and reshape us.

FOR REFLECTION OR DISCUSSION

1. The chapter discusses the five components of biblical lament: calling out to God, complaining to God, bringing requests to God, remembering who God is, and praising God. Which of these components do you find most challenging or uncomfortable? Why?
2. Choose one of the psalms of lament (Psalm 13, 22, 31, 42, 88, and many others) and pray through it each day this week using lectio divina. Pay attention to how the psalmist expresses their emotions, questions, and hopes to God. Journal about how this practice impacts your own prayer life and your perspective on your suffering.
3. Set aside time this week to write your own lament using the five components as a guide. Begin by calling out to God, expressing your honest emotions and complaints. Bring your requests to God, remembering who he is and his faithfulness in the past. End with a statement of praise or trust even if you don't feel it fully. Share your lament with a trusted friend or spiritual mentor.
4. Given that the Psalms were originally songs, can you think of any lament songs (for example, hymns sung in minor keys) your church sings that express real pain and hope? If you

don't know any, look up Martin Luther's "From the Depths of Woe" and consider learning it. How might it help Christians to more regularly sing songs of lament?

FURTHER READING

Mark Vroegop, *Dark Clouds, Deep Mercy: Discovering the Grace of Lament* (Crossway, 2019).

Michael Card, *A Sacred Sorrow: Reaching Out to God in the Lost Language of Lament* (NavPress, 2014).

J. Todd Billings, *Rejoicing in Lament: Wrestling with Incurable Cancer and Life in Christ* (Brazos, 2015).

Nicholas Wolterstorff, *Lament for a Son* (Eerdmans, 1987).

SEVEN

SURRENDER

I realized I need to just surrender this to God because I can't physically do anything about it. And like, "God, do whatever you want to do because there's nothing I can do." . . . It was a moment of surrender and letting go and trusting that God was God. . . . It was actually really freeing, this moment of surrender.

Karina, cancer survivor

A prayer commonly known as the Serenity Prayer may sound familiar if you've had any exposure to Alcoholics Anonymous (AA). Long ago AA adopted a version of this prayer, and it is now recited in unison at the end of each meeting. But this prayer was not originally crafted for struggling alcoholics. It is believed to have been written by pastor and theologian Reinhold Niebuhr in 1943 after four years of brutal world war, when it was not yet clear that the Allies would win.[1] The next year it was included in a little booklet that was passed out to soldiers, providing them a concrete way to take the overwhelming burdens they shouldered each day and give them over to God. At the heart of the prayer is surrender to God, recognizing that many, many things that trouble us are completely out of our control—but not out of God's control. It reads:

God, give me grace to accept with serenity
the things that cannot be changed,
Courage to change the things
which should be changed,
and the Wisdom to distinguish
the one from the other.
Living one day at a time,
Enjoying one moment at a time,
Accepting hardship as a pathway to peace,
Taking, as Jesus did,
This sinful world as it is,
Not as I would have it,
Trusting that You will make all things right,
If I surrender to Your will,
So that I may be reasonably happy in this life,
And supremely happy with You forever in the next.
Amen.[2]

Many of us seem to pray a version of the Serenity Prayer offered by Calvin from Bill Watterson's famous comic strip, *Calvin and Hobbes*. Calvin asks Hobbes, "Know what I pray for?"

"What?" Hobbes replies.

"The strength to change what I can, the inability to accept what I can't, and the incapacity to tell the difference."

To which Hobbes responds, "You should lead an interesting life."[3]

That's one way to describe it! When we find ourselves endlessly grasping for control and unable to acknowledge our limitations, we are setting ourselves up for a very "interesting" life of anxiety, rumination, and distress.

This chapter considers the practice of surrender: turning our circumstances over to God in surrender. As with lament, surrender follows Jesus' example and makes us more like him. In the garden, Jesus lamented and he surrendered his own suffering to the Father, saying, "Not my will, but yours be done." And Jesus' surrender of his suffering to God was not a one-time event. Peter notes that Jesus "entrusted himself" to God in the midst of his suffering (1 Peter 2:23). The verb tense used can be translated "kept entrusting" and indicates that this was a deliberate, active choice on Jesus' part. Jesus kept handing over his sufferings to God; he surrendered regularly.

WHAT IS SURRENDER?

We don't want to suffer. If we could escape it, we would. But throughout the bog of the inescapable, we can meet God in a powerful way and relearn a profound truth about ourselves—that, as creatures, we depend on a loving Creator. Surrender is a recognition of that dependence. Even though we can't escape suffering, we can do something active with it: following Jesus' example, we can entrust it to God.

It's easy to be confused about "surrender" because the word is used in several different ways. Sometimes when we talk about surrender, we mean being forced to do something against our will, as when an army has been conquered and must admit defeat to an enemy. At other times, we use "surrender" to mean giving up. A saying is sometimes heard in Christian circles: "Let go and let God." This seems to advise complete passivity on our part. Instead, what needs to change is the *kind* of activity we pursue. We may feel like completely giving up during difficult times, but this is not what we mean by surrender. In this chapter we will use the word to mean a definite and positive spiritual activity, modeled on the life of Jesus, consisting in loving, active, inward yielding to God and God's will in one's life. Let's look at the different elements of this definition.

The most important thing about surrender is the person to whom we are surrendering: God. Surrender occurs in the context of a personal relationship. We're not surrendering to circumstances or to fate, much less to an enemy's army, but to another person—God. In spiritual surrender we yield to God and God's will. Of course, surrender sometimes happens in other relationships as well. In good marriages, for example, partners submit to each other, giving up their own preferences and goals for the sake of the other. This requires trust. But we should absolutely surrender only to God because only God is perfectly trustworthy. And because God is trustworthy, we can accept God's will for our lives.

Surrender is voluntary. In times of war, a city might surrender to a besieging army, or a soldier might surrender to the enemy and become a prisoner of war. These responses are not voluntary. They are coerced, in that the surrender happens only because there are no other options. In fact, the response may be accompanied by bitterness and resentment. But God is not an enemy who is trying to harm us. He is a Father who only and relentlessly wants our good. When we surrender, we are able to do it willingly, because God has initiated the relationship and shown his trustworthiness.

Surrender is done out of love. Surrender is a loving response to who God is. We submit to God and God's will as an expression of love. We let God lead us and we obey him out of love—even when he is leading us through places we would rather not go. Without this loving motivation for yielding to God, our surrender looks a lot more like surrender to an enemy, in which we obey on the outside while resisting on the inside. This is not the kind of surrender modeled by Jesus, which was also inward while outwardly evidenced by obedience.

Surrender is active, not passive. This brings us to the main element that distinguishes spiritual surrender from other kinds of submission: it is an action that involves continued struggle against the brokenness of our world and of our bodies and minds. One participant we interviewed about her cancer experience summarized her approach in this way: "That's the way I am with my cancer. I mean, I cannot do anything about it. I can do what the doctor tells me. I can watch my diet and I could do all these other things. But the bottom line is God is in control, and he knows when it's time." Her surrender to God included participating in treatment and doing all she could to promote her health.

Surrender is not throwing up our hands in despair and deciding we're no longer going to keep fighting, because surrender is active, not passive. Passive giving up is not the way surrender is modeled for us in the Bible. It involves ongoing, active cooperation with God. For example, while we think of Jesus' death as the ultimate act of surrender, he makes it clear that he willed for it to happen. In John 10, Jesus says he lays down his life, and, just to make sure the point was clear, adds, "No one takes it from me, but I lay it down of my own accord" (John 10:18).

Sometimes Christians advocate a kind of passive surrender because they think life here on earth doesn't matter. When bad things happen, they think the Christian goal is to just ignore them. "After all," they say, "only spiritual things matter." Poverty, illness, and injuries are all part of the sinful, material world, so they are inconsequential and there is little point in trying to actively address these material problems.

But this view doesn't align with the teaching of the whole Bible because our bodies are not an afterthought or dispensable. God made them and we worship God with them (1 Corinthians 6:12-20). When those around Jesus and his disciples faced illness and broken bodies, Jesus healed them. The Bible never tells us to endure suffering by pretending it doesn't exist. Jesus came to save us from our sin, but also from our suffering. When Paul experiences his thorn, he pleads with God to remove it. God doesn't, and Paul carries on, but this doesn't mean Paul merely ignores the pain he's experiencing (2 Corinthians 12:7-10). Surrender yields to God and continues to fight against suffering and evil.

ACTIVE SURRENDER

Active surrender was beautifully illustrated by many of the women from historically Black churches whom we interviewed about their experiences with cancer.[4] At the moment of diagnosis, many of them reported responding in almost identical ways: with surrender. But handing their cancer over to God was always paired with an active approach to treatment. As one participant stated, "The cancer was not my issue . . . that was God's issue. That's not my issue. My issue is go to the doctor, do what they say, and follow your instructions. That's my part." Another, after receiving her diagnosis, told the doctor, "Well, just let me know what I need to do. . . . I know God has this under control." These women surrendered, but they continued to do what they could to end their suffering. But such surrendering does not always look the same: one woman described how "surrendering in grief" after the loss of a child's life felt "different in many ways" from the surrender of a person going through cancer. The point is not uniformity of experience, but discovering what it might look like to surrender to God amid one's own particular suffering.

When we surrender to God, we acknowledge that God is in control and we submit to God's will. Theologians sometimes make careful distinctions when talking about God's "will" (revealed, hidden, active, permissive, and so forth). While we don't need to get into all those details here, we can state that God is not the author of sin, so God does not directly will for us to suffer. But in this fallen world, one must also admit that God does will to allow it in our lives. If we don't confess that, then we easily end up with an impotent God who can't, in the end, bring comfort and fulfill trustworthy promises. God expects us to do what we can in the situation—to be active. God is sovereign and we are responsible. This mysterious dynamic, so central to surrender, is true of the entire Christian life. Notice how it shows up in the apostle Paul's words in Philippians 2:12-13: "Continue to work out your salvation with fear and trembling" (in other words, be active), "for it is God who works in you to will and to act in order to fulfill his good purpose." Because God works, we work. So do we work hard because God is the one making it all happen? Yes! God is active and working, and our responsive "working" is possible only because God is already at work. We don't pick between God being active or us being active. The collaborative nature of surrender was evident in the response of one of our study participants to their cancer diagnosis: "For real? Really, God? Okay, let's just get this done. Let's just do it."

FINDING OUR LIVES BY SURRENDERING THEM

Jesus' example and teaching showed his disciples how to surrender to the Father in the midst of suffering. After he told them for the first time that he would suffer and die, he explained to his disciples that they would need to do the same. They would need to take up their crosses and lose their lives for Christ's sake (Matthew 16:21-26). Dying to self does not mean the death of the self. It is not a destruction of oneself or one's identity. God does not desire that we cease existing. Because God loves us, God is eager to put the distorting nature of sin to death in us so that we might be liberated in the Redeemer's life and love. The other side of dying to self is rising again to new life.

Surrender helps us live as we were designed to live—in deep dependence on God. And vice versa: realizing our deep need and dependence on God enables us to surrender. Accordingly, surrender to Jesus helps us suffer well. We found this in one of our studies when we tested the relationship between spiritual surrender and distress in a large online sample of Christians who indicated they had experienced a negative life event in the last six months.[5] In general, we found that the greater the event's severity, the lower people's satisfaction with life was, as might be expected. However, we also found that this connection differed based on their level of spiritual surrender. At high levels of surrender, the severity of the event didn't change their satisfaction with life. So spiritual surrender seems to be very helpful in coping with difficult life events. It allows us to maintain a sense of life as meaningful even when we face severe challenges.

Psychologists have known for a long time that anxiety typically results from feeling both a lack of control over one's circumstances and having a high need to be in control. This anxiety can be debilitating, often taking up considerable head space and making concentrating on ordinary tasks difficult. Some people spend a lot of time in futile attempts to control what is uncontrollable. Surrender in this case enables us to deal with life realistically: we acknowledge what is beyond our control and trust God to be benevolent and sovereign.

One of the strange and unexpected gifts Liz experienced during her cancer was becoming acutely aware of her finitude. The cancer-related problems with her body reminded her of her bodily limitations as she no longer effortlessly did things like sleeping, which she had previously done easily. Her body wasn't cooperating and felt out of her control. Her desire to live and continue being a mother to her children and a wife to her husband also reminded her that she had no control over the outcomes she most desired in this world. And the uncertainties surrounding her treatment, as well as what God was doing in her life, reminded her that she didn't know everything she wanted to know. Although finitude is at times uncomfortable and something we push against, from a theological perspective, it's part of God's created good. We were designed to be finite creatures, created for a certain kind of relationship—a dependent relationship—with a loving, omnipotent, omniscient God. It's easy to lose sight of that reality in our everyday lives.

But suffering can ground us and help us remember our very real limits. And if we are wise, that will lead us to acknowledge what has been true all along: we are not God, and God is!

Surrender to God in the midst of our suffering can help us see the most fundamental truths about ourselves and about God.

When we embrace our finitude, we also develop intellectual humility, acknowledging there are things we don't understand and things we simply don't know. In one of our qualitative studies with cancer survivors, we divided people into two groups: one in which people expressed some kind of spiritual struggle, and one in which people did not.[6] We then looked for any pervasive differences between those groups, and we found that the presence of intellectual humility seemed to be a protective factor against spiritual struggle. These participants expressed humility by stating that they didn't know why they had cancer, but God did. For example, one participant said,

> God has brought me through this cancer for a reason. And I don't understand it. I don't really have an answer as to why I think I got cancer. But do I have a closer relationship now with God? Yes. . . . Do I understand where my home really lies? Yes. . . . It's not going to matter because in the end I'm going to be with the Lord. . . . What I think I'm going to need to understand may not be that important when you get there. And it won't matter.

In another qualitative study, this time with women from historically Black churches, we found that their intellectual humility made possible a kind of spiritual surrender in which they entrusted their cancer to God.[7] In this study we separated the women into a group that showed substantial distress at the time of the cancer diagnosis and those who showed little distress. The presence of spiritual surrender is what distinguished these two groups.

PATHWAYS TO SURRENDER

Choosing to follow Jesus in the first place is a kind of surrender. We also surrender in an ongoing way through daily choices and actions. As Paul said, "I die daily" (1 Corinthians 15:31 KJV). Several activities support our efforts to surrender. Prayer and lament help us turn our troubles over to God and continue to resist unwanted circumstances. Lament doesn't approach suffering passively but asks God to change the circumstances while accepting the outcome even if he does not (Daniel 3:18).

We can also practice surrendering in the small things so we can more easily surrender in the big things.[8] Whether we're currently experiencing hardship or not, we can receive small, daily annoyances as opportunities to seek God and to surrender. Such practice can be preparation, helping us in the present even as we are also being equipped for future challenges. When we lose our keys, are faced with annoying drivers on the road, or confront a clogged toilet—again!—we can practice handing the situation over to God while also doing what we can to fix it. We can avoid frustration or despair and seek to meet Jesus in the midst of our circumstances.

We can also learn to surrender by growing in intellectual humility and awareness of our limits. One of the people we interviewed about his cancer journey initially struggled with the idea of God's goodness. When asked how this was resolved, he said,

> He can do anything that he wants at his time in his way, and it's not at my direction, at my bargaining, at my pain, at my whining, at my anything. It's up to God and he'll take me when he wants to take me and he'll cure me when he wants to cure me and he won't cure me when he doesn't want to cure me, and that's okay. So I go back to the first

> commandment, that if I can really follow the first commandment and make God my only God. Not my intelligence, not my ability to read a cure on the internet, not my ability to find someone else who got cured and if I do what he does then I'll get cured. If I can let all of that go and just make God God, then everything else kind of goes away. And I can lead the rest of my life breathing, walking, in communion with [God]; it's very nice.

This man's spiritual surrender involved intellectual humility, which our colleague Kent Dunnington defines as "glad intellectual dependence on God."[9] This perspective recognizes our finitude, especially in regard to the outcomes and purposes of the suffering, while also acknowledging the other side of the coin, that God does know and is in control of the outcomes and has loving purposes for our suffering. Rather than demanding to know answers, one of our participants said, "I can just give it to God: 'I don't understand this. Is there something you want me to know, and if there is, could you tell me?' Maybe he doesn't want me to know. . . . I guess when I get to heaven he'll tell me why." Instead of doubting God's purpose, this participant accepted the presence of an unknown plan while simultaneously expressing the desire for its eventual manifestation, patiently searching for purpose.

Finally, to surrender, we may need to abandon some of our beliefs about how the world works. For example, some of our participants gave up their belief in the "justice" of this current world when they surrendered spiritually. One woman said, "The 'why me?' to me is very selfish, because it should be 'why not me?' I'm not any better than anybody else in this earth. . . . Who are we to think that?" She went on to tie this to her original spiritual struggle with God's justice: "I was raised that if you make good choices you have fewer consequences, and I was mad because that's not true. I think that was the hardest one to take." Another woman described her resolution as follows: "I just came to a place where, we're in a world where it's not perfect. We're not in heaven, and things happen." The next world will be just; the current one is not.

THE GIFTS OF SURRENDER

Our research collaborator Jamie Aten tells of his experience being diagnosed with stage four colon cancer at the age of thirty-five in his book *A Walking Disaster*.[10] One day, months into his chemotherapy, Jamie dragged himself outside in the winter snow to take out the trash, all the while struggling with God about his cancer in an attempt to understand and control God. After making his way slowly back inside, exhausted by the small household chore, he found himself dropping to his knees beside his bed. His struggling with God gave way to another prayer: "If I'm not okay, please take care of my wife and my daughters."[11] In that prayer he acknowledged that he didn't know what God's will was and couldn't manipulate God to do his bidding. Yet in that moment, Jamie also felt a deep sense that he could trust God regardless of the outcome. The result was an experience of peace and quiet confidence in God's goodness and reliability: a spiritual surrender. Jamie emphasized that there was nothing passive about this surrender; deciding to trust God was a willful act of obedience.

Surrender brings peace in the midst of the chaotic storms of life. We're held in the hands of the one who holds the world. One of our participants described the comfort, peace, and closeness to God she experienced when she "put her life in God's hands." Surrender brings freedom from fruitless striving and crippling anxiety. When you have died to yourself, the old patterns of your life no longer have dominion over you.

As Jamie experienced, suffering often confronts us with our limitations. Some situations in life are outside our control and some don't have resolutions. Challenges such as chronic illness or the death of a loved one can't be resolved. Fortunately, when circumstances are outside our control, we can be confident that everything is in God's control. Even better, this all-powerful God loves us and is for us. He invites us to turn to him in surrender.

FOR REFLECTION OR DISCUSSION

1. The chapter suggests that practicing surrender in small, daily challenges can prepare us for surrendering in the face of more significant suffering.
   - What are some areas of your life where you currently struggle to surrender to God?
   - When you experience daily annoyances, things that didn't go your way, practice praying, "I turn this over to you, God," or "I surrender ______________ to you. I trust in your love for me." You can approach this practice as a kind of breath prayer where each breath is a prayer that can be repeated.
   - In prayer, express your trust that God is working in the midst of difficulties you face.
2. Write your own version of the Serenity Prayer, personalizing it to your specific circumstances and challenges. Pray this prayer each morning (or at another time of day), asking God

to grant you the grace to accept what you cannot change, the courage to change what you can, and the wisdom to discern between the two.

3. Reflect on the following quote by C. S. Lewis. How does it help you understand what it means to surrender to God? "Now the proper good of a creature is to surrender itself to its Creator—to enact intellectually, volitionally, and emotionally, that relationship which is given in the mere fact of its being a creature. The creature's illusion of self-sufficiency must, for the creature's sake, be shattered."[12]
4. Using lectio divina, reflect on the following passages: Psalm 55, especially v. 22; Psalm 31:5; Proverbs 3:1-8; Luke 9:21-27; Luke 22:39-42.

FURTHER READING

David G. Benner, *Surrender to Love: Discovering the Heart of Christian Spirituality* (InterVarsity Press, 2015).

Dallas Willard, *Life Without Lack: Living in the Fullness of Psalm 23* (Zondervan, 2019).

Kelly M. Kapic, *You're Only Human: How Your Limits Reflect God's Design and Why That's Good News* (Brazos, 2022).

Andrew Murray, *Absolute Surrender* (Aneko Press, [1895] 2017).

EIGHT

FORGIVENESS

I think I can forgive my first husband, who was very abusive, because I can see the path he's taken and I just have sympathy for him. . . . I don't have any negative feelings for him anymore, and I don't ever wish anything bad for him. In fact, I've always wished that he would find peace.

Leah, cancer survivor

When Gary Ridgway, known as the Green River Killer, was sentenced for his murder of forty-eight women, the victims' families were each allowed to address their loved one's murderer. As you might imagine, their statements were filled with hatred and desires for revenge—until Bob Rule, father of one of the victims, stood and faced the killer. He looked at Ridgway and said, "Mr. Ridgway, there are people here who hate you. I'm not one of them. I forgive you for what you've done. You've made it difficult to live up to what I believe, and that is what God says to do, and that is forgive, and he doesn't say to forgive just certain people; he says forgive all. So you are forgiven."

Ridgway, who had been stoic to that point, began to cry.

Even when our suffering is not caused by human failure, forgiveness may still be a necessary meaning-making practice. We don't have to forgive illnesses or losses from natural disasters, such as fires, earthquakes, and tornadoes, as they are not caused by humans. But whether the distressing life event is caused by another human or not, the reality is that as we stumble down the paths of our suffering, we encounter fallen humans who often respond in less-than-ideal ways.

WHY FORGIVE?

Although Liz's cancer was not caused by anyone else, people sometimes (and usually unintentionally) added to her distress: people she counted on who seemed to forget her in her time of need, people who responded insensitively to news of her diagnosis by telling her stories of friends who had died of cancer, a doctor whose actions caused a long delay in her treatment, insurance representatives who made mistakes that required long hours on the phone. These hurts accumulated even amid a treatment that went remarkably smoothly! Our daily lives and trials present many opportunities to exercise forgiveness.

Sometimes, as with Bob Rule, the actions of others cause our suffering. A person filled with hatred attacks without cause. A drunk driver causes the death of a loved one. An inattentive and sleep-deprived doctor botches the surgery and causes a lasting disability. A careless smoker causes a fire that destroys a home. In such cases, forgiveness is a critical meaning-making practice, absolutely essential for arriving at a good place.

We need to practice forgiveness for two reasons. First, few options exist for resolving situations where we have been injured as the result of the actions of others. Some people try to avoid the person or situation, but that doesn't lead to any resolution. For resolution, that leaves either revenge or forgiveness. And revenge—aside from being immoral!—is only a superficial solution. In reality, revenge contributes to an unending sequence in which aggression leads to more aggression, hurts contribute to more hurts, and the cycle continues on and on.

Forgiveness disrupts and stops the cycle. Forgiveness allows the process of healing to move forward. Research shows that while in the short-term revenge might feel good, in the long term, people focused on revenge experience more depression and continued anger than people who forgive, which can lead to deteriorating well-being and life satisfaction.[1] In contrast, forgiveness frees us from the chains of unforgiveness, hatred, and anger that bind us to the transgressor. Forgiveness allows us to change the meaning of the event we are struggling to forgive. As Christian psychologist Lewis Smedes once said, "To forgive is to set a prisoner free and discover that the prisoner was you."[2]

Jesus taught the centrality of forgiveness. He also modeled forgiveness, extending mercy even under the most extreme of circumstances. When we follow Jesus' example in how he faced suffering, and when we walk the path of suffering in obedience to what Jesus taught, we must do it with the willingness to forgive. How is that possible? We can forgive because we have been forgiven.

FORGIVING AS JESUS FORGAVE

Forgiveness is at the heart of our faith. Christianity is all about God forgiving us. God offered forgiveness when we didn't deserve it. God offered forgiveness when we hadn't asked for it—in fact, while we were enemies (Romans 5:6-10). And God, in Christ, offered forgiveness in a way that cost him his life. Without Jesus' death, God's forgiveness would not have been possible. What do we give up when we forgive? Our pride? Our ability to nurse our grudges, to cultivate our victimhood?

Jesus taught, illustrated, and modeled forgiveness. First, Jesus taught us to pray, "Forgive us our debts, as we also have forgiven our debtors" (Matthew 6:12). Of the many parts of the Lord's Prayer, this verse is the only one Jesus chose to explain further: "For if you forgive other people when they sin against you, your heavenly Father will also forgive you. But if you do not forgive others their sins, your Father will not forgive your sins" (Matthew 6:14-15). Jesus takes our willingness to forgive very, very seriously. When we are willing to forgive, we demonstrate the repentant heart that comes from having truly received forgiveness (Luke 7:47). If we take seriously the enormity of our offense against God—the kind of offense that required the death of Jesus—then what others do to us pales in comparison.

Jesus illustrates the contrast between God's forgiveness of us and what we need to forgive in others in Matthew 18. Peter first asks if forgiving someone seven times is enough—probably thinking he's being quite generous in this number (v. 21). After all, the rabbinic teachings of the time said three times was enough. Jesus' response shows the inadequacy of Peter's offer. Not seven times, but seventy times seven (v. 22)! His point is not that we should keep track until we have reached 490 instances of forgiveness and then we're off the hook. Rather, we should never reach the end of our willingness to forgive.

To explain, Jesus tells the story of the two debtors (Matthew 18:23-35). The master forgives his servant a debt of over a billion dollars. Yet this servant turns around and refuses to forgive his fellow servant the equivalent of a hundred days' wages. No matter how difficult it is to forgive someone who has harmed us, when we are faced with how much we have been forgiven and how costly that forgiveness was, isn't our heart moved to at least try to forgive? If it isn't, perhaps we have not yet fully experienced the reality of God's forgiveness.

Finally, Jesus modeled forgiveness, even in extreme circumstances. Hanging on the cross, he paused in the midst of excruciating pain to intercede for his murderers, praying, "Father, forgive them, for they do not know what they are doing" (Luke 23:34). God in Christ secures our forgiveness and clearly demonstrates its radical and transformative power and grace. Followers of Christ who have experienced such divine forgiveness also follow Jesus' example, extending forgiveness even to those who do not deserve it.

WHAT FORGIVENESS IS NOT

Unfortunately, many people are confused about what forgiveness is, which makes trying to forgive someone challenging. To define forgiveness, we must first distinguish it from several similar actions.

Forgiveness is not trivializing the offense. Sometimes we respond to an apology with phrases like, "It was nothing." That is not forgiveness. If "it was nothing," then there is nothing to forgive. Forgiveness takes seriously the wrong that was done. It doesn't downplay or belittle the offense. Our model for forgiveness is God. Did God trivialize sin in forgiving us? By no means. To forgive, Christ first took our sin upon himself, "nailing it to the cross"—and then he forgave (Colossians 2:13-14). The cost of forgiveness shows the depth of sin. True forgiveness recognizes the severity of the offense and its consequences. Forgiveness does not require us to make light of real hurt, abuse, or pain.

Forgiveness is not forgetting. Many of us wish that we could, as the saying goes, "forgive and forget." Unfortunately, we can't selectively develop amnesia for events in our lives. In fact, there's value in not forgetting. When we remember, we can also learn from our experiences, increasing our ability to navigate challenging situations and people even while gaining wisdom. Granting forgiveness does not rob us of the gift of learning from the past. However, while we can't forget, forgiveness can change our relationships with our memories. The memories of the difficult events in our lives slowly lose their grip on our hearts and emotions. When we forgive, the memories don't have the same destructive power over us that they used to have.

Forgiveness is not reconciliation. Maybe the most significant misunderstanding about forgiveness is that it always involves a reconciled relationship with the person who has hurt us. However, when these two distinct realities are unhelpfully combined, we often end up with a dangerous distortion. Instead, forgiveness is something that happens inside one person. It involves cognitive, emotional, and behavioral changes within the person who has been wronged. Forgiveness can be extended to people with whom you've never been in a relationship—even people you've never met. It can be extended to people who are dead. It can be extended to people who have not repented of what they have done. Forgiveness happens inside of you.

Reconciliation involves two people within the context of a relationship. It depends not on one person's actions but on the actions of the two people in the relationship. You can extend forgiveness, but the other person may not receive it, making reconciliation impossible. Forgiveness, both given and received, is essential to true reconciliation. But even that is not enough for reconciliation. Hurt violates our trust. A person doesn't magically become trustworthy after having been forgiven. Trust needs to be earned. Forgiveness makes reconciliation possible but not inevitable. Forgiveness changes our hearts so that we may become open to attempting reconciliation. But relationships—especially intimate relationships—are built on mutuality and trustworthiness. Depending on the situation, reconciliation may best develop slowly and gradually as trustworthiness is demonstrated over time. God calls us to love others, even our enemies. But we are not commanded to open ourselves up to needless exploitation.

Consider, for example, the typical pattern in abusive relationships. When a woman has been abused by her husband, forgiveness will allow her to move on from the abuse. But suppose she thinks forgiveness involves reconciliation. In that case, she will likely fall into the trap of perpetuating the well-documented abuse cycle, in which the husband begs for forgiveness, but soon returns to the abusive behavior. Some might argue that the loving action in that situation is reconciling with the husband. But if love involves doing what is best for someone else, how is enabling the perpetrator never to face the consequences of his actions a loving thing? Forgiveness is always a good idea. Reconciliation is sometimes a bad and even an unloving thing to do. We must keep these two distinct.

It's very good news that forgiveness is not the same as reconciliation. If it were, then we would be held hostage to our past by someone else's behavior. If the other person refused to reconcile, we would never be able to forgive and move on. Thankfully, while the other person's cooperation is necessary for reconciliation, it is not required for forgiveness. Forgiveness is something you can choose to do. Such forgiveness can be a key element in helping us through the meaning-making process amid our suffering.

THE BENEFITS OF FORGIVING OTHERS

Fifty years ago, there was virtually no psychological research on forgiveness. It was seen as something in the religious realm and consequently inappropriate for psychological study. That changed when one Christian psychologist, Ev Worthington, decided to make the risky career choice to focus his research on forgiveness.[3] Unsurprisingly, he found out that forgiveness was good for people, as well as being foundational to happy relationships. Thankfully, there are now hundreds of quality studies on forgiveness. These academic studies show the multitude of benefits people receive when they forgive.

The benefits of forgiveness extend beyond the spiritual realm. Researchers studying tens of thousands of people have consistently found that those who forgive more readily enjoy better mental health—they're happier, more satisfied with life, experience more positive emotions, and struggle less with negative ones.[4] The physical benefits are equally striking. People who practice forgiveness have better overall health, and their hearts especially benefit. Studies show lower blood pressure and healthier heart rhythms among those who forgive, which makes sense when you consider how chronic anger and resentment create ongoing stress that literally wears down our cardiovascular system.[5] Unresolved anger is bad for the heart!

Furthermore, when we forgive in the context of our personal relationships, we open the door to maintaining and deepening those relationships. Fascinating research from Japan reveals there are actually two types of forgiveness: "true forgiveness" and "hollow forgiveness." When people forgive primarily to get something for themselves—to reduce their own stress, look good to others, or protect their self-image—they experience only surface-level benefits. But when people forgive out of genuine care for the relationship—because they want to stay connected to someone, feel sympathy for them, or simply want to show grace—they experience much deeper healing and greater satisfaction with the outcome.[6] This distinction illuminates something profound about the nature of forgiveness. Here we discover a transformative path through suffering: when we strive to forgive as Jesus forgave, allowing God's love for us to flow out from us to others as we extend forgiveness and grace, we're not just following a moral command—we're participating in the very relational dynamic that brings the deepest healing to our hearts and relationships.

FORGIVING OURSELVES

Sometimes it's not others we have to forgive but ourselves. In our interviews with cancer patients, we spoke to people who faced significant regret over their past actions. They had delayed getting the mammogram or seeking an appointment for their unexplained pain. They had hurt others in ways that could not be easily remedied. Sometimes they faced a terminal diagnosis with the sense that much of their lives had been lived in meaningless ways. Forgiving ourselves is often needed as we seek to put together the pieces of our suffering journeys in meaningful ways.

While forgiving others is emphasized throughout the New Testament, self-forgiveness doesn't appear in Scripture. At least it doesn't show up with that name. Yet the basic idea flows from biblical teaching. God in Christ has forgiven us. Jesus paid the debt of our sin. When we hang on to the burden of our offenses against others and against ourselves, when we allow guilt, shame, and self-blame to permeate our lives and undermine our relationships, aren't we refusing to accept and internalize God's gift of forgiveness? The apostle John seemed to understand the challenge of self-forgiveness when he wrote, "This is how we know that we belong to the truth and how we set our hearts at rest in his presence: If our hearts condemn us, we know that God is greater than our hearts, and he knows everything" (1 John 3:19-20). When we have difficulty forgiving ourselves, we can turn to God and rest in God's truth that there is no condemnation for those who are in Christ Jesus (Romans 8:1).

As with forgiveness, we need to be careful how we think about self-forgiveness. Self-forgiveness is not letting ourselves off the hook, thinking what we did wasn't so bad, or refusing to take responsibility for our actions. Self-forgiveness is not wondering why everyone else is making such a big deal out of what we did. It is not about creating excuses for our behavior or desires. Instead, it begins with carefully searching our heart, asking God to show us our hidden sins, and confessing wherever we fall short. We accept responsibility for what we have done.[7] And genuine self-forgiveness leads to feeling and showing regret and remorse, as well as doing what we can to make restitution for the harm we have caused.

As with forgiving others, research shows that self-forgiveness has a number of benefits.[8] It reduces feelings of shame even as it also predicts physical health and psychological well-being. In fact, the relationship between self-forgiveness and psychological well-being is even stronger than that between other-forgiveness and psychological well-being. Furthermore, self-forgiveness is related to better relationship outcomes. This is probably because the shame and guilt associated with a lack of self-forgiveness may cause us to pull away from others and hide. A mark of shame includes the tendency to retreat, isolate, and soak in embarrassment. This drives us away from God and others, which is the opposite of the gospel. Those negative emotions are barriers to our ability to love and receive love. We need vulnerability, welcome, forgiveness, and grace, all of which are received only when we allow transparency and honesty about our shortcomings, both with ourselves and others. This takes us back to the central place of forgiveness.

THE NUTS AND BOLTS OF FORGIVENESS

Forgiveness is crucial. Yet of all the meaning-making practices we suggest, forgiveness may be the most difficult. This is because forgiveness involves relinquishing feelings—feelings of hurt, anger, and betrayal. And we don't have direct control over our emotions. Because of this, it's helpful to think about forgiveness as both a decision and a process. We can control our decision to forgive. We can choose to imitate Christ in this way. This decision won't resolve all of the difficult emotions immediately, but it does begin an intentional process of change. Sometimes people will say that they are not yet emotionally ready to forgive; they don't feel like forgiving and can't move forward. But waiting to feel forgiveness before deciding to forgive keeps us stuck in the past and in feelings that may or may not change with time.

Christian psychologist Ev Worthington developed one of the most extensively researched pathways for forgiving others. He proposed a five-step process individuals can take to work toward forgiveness: it is known as the REACH model of forgiveness.[9] We will briefly review the model here but recommend that you visit his website listed in the Further Reading section at the end of the chapter for more details.

R is for "recall the hurt." Sometimes people mistakenly believe that forgiveness requires minimizing or disregarding the hurt they have experienced. The opposite is true. Forgiving is a healing process that takes time. It requires a clear recognition of the wrong that has been done and its many negative consequences. In this step, spend time carefully considering the event and the ways it has influenced your life. This is difficult, and, understandably, you may be reluctant to engage in this step. But for forgiveness to be comprehensive, you need to take account of all the hurts you are forgiving. Take some time to consider the impact on your life.

E is for "empathize." Try to understand where the person who hurt you was coming from rather than judging it from the vantage point of your own experience. Try to identify with the life circumstances and events that shaped the person and led them to do what they did. When someone hurts us, it is easy to caricature them as all bad and barely human. We might think about them entirely in terms of what they did. This subtly dehumanizes them. Forgiveness becomes more possible when we recognize that the other person is flawed, fallible, sinful, weak—but also damaged and hurt. Ironically, it's only when we recognize the other person as human, both made in God's image and yet profoundly affected by this fallen world, that we can hold them responsible for what they did. If we dehumanize them, reducing them to a demon or animal, we also need to absolve them of responsibility; after all, animals don't have morality, and it's the character of demons to do wrong things! It's only when we recognize that we are more alike than different that we can have compassion for the other person and move forward with forgiveness. Empathy is not condoning what the other person did but an attempt to understand where the person was coming from.

A is for "altruistic gift." Next, we act on the empathy we've developed for the person who hurt us and offer them the gift of forgiveness. We don't offer this gift because the person deserves it or has earned it. It is altruistic. It comes from a place of humility, based on the recognition that we also have benefited from the forgiveness of others and, ultimately, from the forgiveness of God. Ephesians 4:32 encourages us to imitate God, being "kind and compassionate to one another, forgiving each other, just as in Christ God forgave you."

C is for "commit." While forgiveness is a process, it also involves a decision. Solidify and commit to the decision to forgive. When you find yourself struggling with hurt and anger, the commitment will be an anchor you can return to again and again. Make your commitment as concrete and memorable as possible. You can do this by sharing your decision with someone, writing a certificate of forgiveness, or even writing a letter of forgiveness to the person who has hurt you—whether or not you actually send it.

H is for "hold on to forgiveness." This is the last and longest step in the process. It involves working on the process of forgiveness for the long haul. Memories of the hurtful event will likely surface after you have made the commitment to forgive. This does not mean you haven't forgiven. Unforgiveness happens when we nurse the hurt feelings, ruminate on the events, and fantasize about revenge. You can choose instead to respond in ways that deepen your forgiveness. You can distract yourself from ruminating. You can remind yourself you have forgiven the person. You can think through the earlier steps of the forgiveness process again.

How? Liz has a friend who suffered substantial career setbacks because of a coworker. Since they work for the same company, her friend occasionally sees this individual. Liz once asked her how she coped with this situation. Her friend said, "Well, I pray for him. I pray that his day will go well, that he will be successful at his job, that his family will prosper. And when I do that, I find that God is also changing my heart toward him." This coworker will never be a friend, nor will Liz's friend willingly trust him again—he hasn't demonstrated that trustworthiness. But her negative feelings toward him have—with occasional flare-ups—been resolved, and she is even able to wish him well. But to arrive at this place, Liz's friend had to make choices every time the negative feelings came back. Forgiveness is not simply a one-time event.

There is much more to say about forgiveness than we have been able to outline in one chapter. If you are struggling to forgive, we hope you'll use some of the excellent resources listed below. The decision to forgive is essential, but remember that forgiveness is also a process. Be patient with yourself and persevere in following through with forgiveness. In doing so, you will be reflecting the forgiving heart of God and following more closely in Jesus' footsteps. You will be able to experience more deeply the fellowship of his suffering, "forgiving each other, just as in Christ God forgave you" (Ephesians 4:32).

FOR REFLECTION OR DISCUSSION

1. Consider the REACH model of forgiveness presented in the chapter. Which step do you find most challenging? Why? How might you work on overcoming this challenge?
2. Reflect on the concept of self-forgiveness discussed in the chapter. Are there areas in your life where you struggle to forgive yourself? How might reflecting on God's forgiveness help you in this process?
3. Reflect on the following passages using lectio divina: Matthew 18:21-35; Colossians 3:12-14; Matthew 6:9-15; Ephesians 4:31-32; Psalm 103:1-5, 8-12.

FURTHER READING

Everett L. Worthington, "REACH Forgiveness of Others," Everett Worthington (website), copyright 2025, www.evworthington-forgiveness.com/reach-forgiveness-of-others.

Everett L. Worthington, *Moving Forward: Six Steps to Forgiving Yourself and Breaking Free from the Past* (WaterBrook, 2013).

Lewis B. Smedes, *Forgive and Forget: Healing the Hurts We Don't Deserve* (Harper & Row, 1984).

NINE

GRATITUDE

I remember one night, I think I was mid-chemo, I was lying in bed and I was not feeling well, and I just had this profound sense of gratitude. I was like, "God, thank you that our bodies can heal. Thank you for Western medicine. Thank you for my family. Thank you for my friends. Thank you for the sun outside." I just was in this place of deep gratitude. . . . I had this sense of all this stuff to be thankful for, and that really guided me through a lot of the harder moments.

Pablo, cancer survivor

Paul instructed the Thessalonians to "give thanks in all circumstances; for this is God's will for you in Christ Jesus" (1 Thessalonians 5:18). He also told the Ephesians to "be filled with the Spirit . . . always giving thanks to God the Father for everything" (Ephesians 5:18-20). Did he really mean "all" and "everything"? What about when we're suffering? Are we supposed to thank God when our world is crumbling around us?

Two young sisters decided to take Paul's instruction seriously in the most extreme of circumstances (actually, one of them decided and the other came along grudgingly). When Betsie and Corrie Ten Boom were moved to a new barracks during their imprisonment in a Nazi concentration camp, a room notorious for being flea-ridden, Betsie wanted to apply what they had read from Paul right away: "'Give thanks in all circumstances! That's what we can do. We can start right now to thank God for every single thing about this new barracks!' . . . 'Thank You,' Betsie went on serenely, 'for the fleas and for—.'"

Her sister Corrie wasn't impressed. She writes, "The fleas! This was too much. 'Betsie, there's no way even God can make me grateful for a flea.'"

Betsie responded in the way that bossy older sisters do: "Give thanks in all circumstances," she quoted. "It doesn't say, 'in pleasant circumstances.'"

Corrie continues, "And so we stood between piers of bunks and gave thanks for fleas. But this time I was sure Betsie was wrong."[1]

Corrie's response to her overbearing older sister is relatable. How could they be thankful for yet another aggravation in the midst of awful circumstances? God has a sense of humor, though, and Corrie did end up being thankful for the fleas. They ensured that the guards never came near their cell, and the sisters were free to carry out prohibited Bible studies.

GIFTS, GRATITUDE, AND . . . SUFFERING?

As we enter this exploration of gratitude, we need to be clear about some basics: our holy God does not like evil, and suffering is lamentable. Sin and human suffering are not the way things are supposed to be for God's image bearers. Those who are victims of abuse, violence, and devastating trauma may especially need to hear this. God did not create sin (which is a twisting of his good creation), and he does not delight in our suffering (which grows out of the brokenness of this fallen world). When we talk about gratitude in the context of suffering, we need to avoid any kind of glorification of evil. We should avoid any hint that suffering is a good thing we should masochistically seek out.

Neither does exercising gratitude in the midst of suffering mean putting a positive spin on it or insisting it's not really all that bad. Going down that path makes us liars or at least terribly naive, which often leads to hurting rather than helping people. Furthermore, learning to be grateful doesn't mean we stop working against what is wrong in the world, nor do we stop lamenting; gratitude is not a replacement for honestly expressing our suffering to God. It's worth noting that Paul's instructions were to be thankful in, not for, all circumstances (1 Thessalonians 5:18).

And yet God can meet us in special ways in the midst of our various experiences of suffering and even graciously give us gifts for which we can be thankful in and through our suffering (for example, see the story of Joseph). God provides daily grace to meet us in our hard times. When we see what God is doing and has done—and maybe, like Betsie Ten Boom, even before we see what God is doing!—we can respond to God in gratitude "in all circumstances." Our journeys of suffering can provide opportunities to thank God for the gifts we have been given along the hard road to glory. Stephanie, one of our cancer survivor participants, expressed a similar idea: "I also felt very loved that God would care enough about me to allow me to go through this. Not that he gave me cancer—I don't believe that. But that he cared enough to say, 'I'm going to dig a little deeper with you, and we're going to go on a journey.' He cared deeply about me, and I was just feeling that God was there, God was present."

The words *graciously, grace, gratitude,* and *gift* all share the same root—*charis*—in Greek. In fact, *charis* literally means "gift" and is often translated "grace." There is a strong link between grace and gratitude. God shows grace in all the gifts he gives to us, including salvation, but also every other good and perfect gift in our lives (James 1:17).[2] Gratitude is a response to grace. Again and again we find these two words linked in our Bibles. God is always giving to us abundantly, not by calling evil good, but by being present with us and for us even amid the hurt and pain. When we are grateful, we are training ourselves to see God's grace, the unearned gift of God's presence and love "in all circumstances." And we are reminded that this suffering will not be our eternal experience.

Letitia found that one of the gifts of her time in treatment for cancer was becoming more grateful. She said, "I think I appreciate things more. I don't want to waste time. I want to appreciate each day. I want to be kinder. I'm more empathetic. I'm more grateful. I try to practice gratitude every day. Even during treatment, I tried to practice gratitude. . . . I've found that gratitude is transformative. If you wake up and say, 'What am I grateful for today?' instead of, 'What's going to go wrong today?' it changes how you look at the day."

Gratitude acknowledges givers, gifts, and our gain from what we've been given. Suffering enhances our connection with each of these three elements and can grow gratitude in us.

THE GIVER GIVES HIMSELF

Writing to the church in Corinth, Paul recounts a source of ongoing suffering. The language he uses to describe his suffering is graphic: "A thorn"—a barb or fishhook—"was given me in the flesh" (2 Corinthians 12:7 ESV). Commentators typically identify the Greek word translated "was given" as a divine passive. Clearly, God could have stopped it, and since he didn't, this means God allowed this to happen and was the indirect cause of Paul's hardship. It was an unwanted "gift." Paul wasn't seeking out suffering, and he didn't just fatalistically give up. Like Jesus in Gethsemane, he pleaded with God three times to remove his suffering. Also like Jesus, Paul's suffering continued despite his prayers and his strong faith in God.

Christians throughout the centuries have had many questions about Paul's thorn. What was it? Dozens of guesses have been proposed. Instead of explaining, Paul focuses on the main point: God met him in his suffering. God spoke to Paul, reminding him that "my grace is sufficient for you, for my power is made perfect in weakness" (2 Corinthians 12:9). This is the only place where Jesus' words to Paul are reported directly in Paul's writings. As with Job, God brings comfort to Paul through direct communication. This also contrasts with the revelations Paul describes in the preceding verses. He doesn't report the content of those either. This revelation is more important.

Paul next says he exults despite his weaknesses, "so that Christ's power may rest on me" (2 Corinthians 12:9). The word picture of "rest on" is the same concept as God's appearance with his people in the tabernacle and in the temple. It is the way God became "God with us" in the incarnation of Jesus (John 1:14). In the midst of his suffering, Jesus took up residence in Paul's life. Jesus moved in to Paul's home.

All the practices we have discussed in this book have this in common: we can grow in deeper relationship with Jesus through our suffering. Ultimately, gifts for which we are grateful are not about the object that is given but the strengthening of relationship with the one who has given them. Even gifts we don't want can do that.

Much to Jason's surprise, a friend who suffered severe daily back pain, migraines, and resulting sleeplessness was not in a hurry to be healed. Why? Because he worried that the special relationship with Christ he had developed in the context of his suffering would disappear. He saw his pain as a kind of gift for which he was grateful. This may seem extreme, but many Christians have reported similar experiences.[3] Unfortunately, the special sweetness of loving connection to Jesus can also be missed during our suffering. Of the ten lepers who were healed, only one returned with gratitude to Jesus (Luke 17:11-19). The other nine missed out on the main thing, even though they were healed. Both suffering and healing can take people further away from Jesus. Both can bring them closer. Gratitude can make the difference, bringing us closer to Jesus in both the good times and the bad (Job 1:21).

GRATITUDE ON THE PATH

Recently Jason's teenaged son came off crutches from a broken ankle and exclaimed, "Isn't it wonderful to be able to walk? I love it!" You know, it really is wonderful to be able to walk. Most of us are fortunate that we never have to think about the wonders of walking. Noticing things we had taken for granted helps gratitude emerge while we are hurting. Losses help us recognize and be grateful for things we've lost and for things we've always had but never noticed. These are gifts in the midst of suffering. When we don't have good things in our lives or when we receive them back, we can realize how wonderful they are. Perhaps it's the ability to breathe after congestion, or the ability to taste once the effects of the drugs have worn off. Suffering provides contrasts that can provoke us to notice gifts God has already given us.

Another way suffering prompts gratitude is that it brings huge disruptions to our normal routines. We may have to go about our lives very differently when tragedy strikes. We may be prevented from working or going to school; our time can be punctuated with doctor's visits and treatment. When suffering changes our plans, we have the opportunity to savor parts of our lives we neglected or hadn't noticed. Disruption of habit can help us become more attuned to beauty or to appreciate our relationships more deeply. If we can't rush past on our way to important business, we may smell, perhaps for the first time, the roses on our path. Ordinary activities to which we never gave much thought, like sipping coffee, can become profound experiences of delight and communion with God and others.

Suffering may also help us become more spiritually attuned. Scripture shows us times when God met and spoke to suffering people in unique and radical ways—perhaps because their suffering caused them to listen to God differently and more attentively. When we notice these gifts, recording them in a journal or sharing them with others helps us express our gratitude. Giving thanks to God for these moments pours delight in God's goodness into our hearts.

Both suffering and gratitude position us to receive.[4] Our world constantly tempts us to believe we have more control over our circumstances and our lives than we do. When we go through stressful life situations, we seek, or have recommended to us, cures for everything that ails us. We may believe we just need another medicine, or therapy, or how-to book, and then we'll put the ship back on course. But eventually we run out of ways to control or fix our current situation, and we are hit with the reality of our finitude. As David Steindl-Rast puts it, "Self-sufficiency is an illusion. And, sooner or later, life shatters every illusion."[5] We see again the spiritual truth of our limits and, if we can receive the reminder of our finitude as a gift, we can be grateful for having the veil removed from our eyes. We have been designed to be dependent on and in relationship with God. Suffering can put us in touch with this fundamental reality.

GAINING PERSPECTIVE BY LOOKING BACK AT OUR JOURNEY

Gifts resulting from the hard things in our lives may not have been gained in any other way. It may take time and perspective to uncover these gifts. But whether or not we have already recognized these gifts, we can be grateful to God that he is working in and through our circumstances. Even the terrible ones.

Many character strengths can be gained only in difficult circumstances. The Bible lists several traits gained through trials: perseverance, character, hope, and maturity (Romans 5:3-4; James 1:2-4). Paul twice repeated that God meant for the thorn to teach him humility. How could courage or patience be cultivated in the absence of hardship? Compassion and creativity, self-control and loyalty—many beautiful human traits are refined by the fire of suffering. When we look back and see how the Holy Spirit has instilled these characteristics in us through the difficulties we have faced, we can be profoundly grateful. As you look at your past difficulties, what good things did you receive from them? How does remembering God's faithful goodness in your past trials strengthen you for your current hardship?

Psychological research helps us understand how gratitude is key to growing in the midst of suffering and how the absence of gratitude can result in stagnation. Psychologist Barbara Fredrickson proposed the "broaden and build" theory of positive emotions, which highlights the benefits gratitude can bring about as a meaning-making practice in the midst of suffering.[6] When we hurt, we often experience anger, sadness, and fear. We call these "negative" emotions because they don't feel good. Negative emotions narrow our focus on the cause of the pain, which is a helpful strategy for fixing the problem. But not all problems are fixable, and negative emotions can get us stuck.

By contrast, positive emotions such as gratitude broaden our viewpoint. They help us gain a bigger perspective to see more of the picture, and they build our capacity to love and serve others.[7] This broadening is associated with ways gratitude builds: It produces positive psychological, intellectual, social, and physical resources, and it results in life satisfaction.[8] In the midst of suffering, gratitude builds our relationship with God: It grows trust in God by helping us see evidence of God's provision and care. Psychological research reveals that gratitude works like a social glue, drawing us closer to the people in our lives and making us feel genuinely connected rather than isolated.[9]

Gratitude does more than just improve our relationships—it changes how we handle life's inevitable challenges. Studies show that grateful people don't just feel better; they cope better, finding creative solutions and bouncing back faster when things go wrong.[10] Perhaps most remarkably, researchers have discovered that gratitude helps us find meaning. It's as if gratitude is a lens that brings the important things into sharper focus while making the trivial stuff fade into the background.[11]

FINDING THE GIFTS IN SUFFERING

Some gifts from God in the context of suffering are easy to find. During Liz's chemotherapy, reactions to the chemo would follow a pattern, with symptoms spiking a couple of days after each infusion, then gradually diminishing until it was time for a new infusion. One of her distinct memories was taking a walk during a "good" day and taking delight in the wonderful, warm sunlight on her face. Another memory was finally being able to enjoy a good cup of coffee after several months in which the metallic taste left over from chemotherapy had made coffee taste terrible. It was easy to find, and be grateful, for these things.

Barb, one of our participants, was more intentional in finding these gifts. She said, "One of the things that I kept doing through the cancer was reminding myself to be grateful. I got a journal, and every day I would write down three things I was grateful for. And some days it was hard. Some days I'd be like, 'I'm grateful for . . . uh . . . this pen I'm writing with?' But the practice of gratitude carried me through. Even on my worst days, when I was feeling horrible physically, I could find something to be thankful for. And that shifted my focus." Keeping a gratitude journal or identifying three good things every day can help us be intentional about finding God's gifts. Sharing with others strengthens this even more. When we hear the gratitude of our loved ones, we're reminded, "I'm grateful for that, too!"

But some gifts are more challenging to identify. Discerning what God is doing in the midst of our hurt can be difficult. While we can be confident that God is in the business of redeeming evil, we are often ignorant of the details. Even though God met Job in a special way, Job never had his questions answered. Understandably, we probably won't give thanks when we're not aware that we've been given something. Our relationship with the giver can't be strengthened if we don't even know there is a giver. Most of us won't receive direct communication from God about our suffering that explains its benefits.

We may assume that biblical figures had it easier than us: They knew what God was doing. Paul had direct communication from God regarding his thorn, which must have been a great comfort to him. But Paul did not report that God told him he was supposed to learn humility. How did he discover that? Through most of his catastrophic life, Joseph did not know what God was doing. How did he come to see that what his brothers meant for evil God meant for good (Genesis 50:20)? God may not have directly told Paul or Joseph these things. They may have been more like us than we think.

How do we wisely discern what God gives us through our trials? We take our suffering to God. We can ask, *God, what are you doing in the midst of my suffering? How are you showing yourself within it?* Like the nine lepers, we might forget to ask this question because we are preoccupied with pleading to have the suffering removed.

We also might ask others to help us discern what God is doing with our suffering. People who love us often see what we don't and may be able to discern God's handiwork in the midst of our hard times. Since our loved ones suffer when we suffer, it is also appropriate to ask what God is doing in our loved ones through the suffering we experience. Paul "boasted" in his suffering, but it is clear in the context that the Corinthians found

Paul's weakness to be shameful. We are often reluctant to share our difficulties because we do not wish to be perceived as weak or an object of pity by those around us. But those around us can help us discern what God is doing in us and through us, not in the absence of our weakness but in its undeniable presence.

Often we don't see good gifts from suffering until much later, when time and perspective broaden our view. Corrie ten Boom found out the role of the fleas during her imprisonment only later, when she was able to discern the patterns of her experiences. Time and perspective, God's voice, the insights of loved ones—all of these illuminate the gifts we've been given on the journey.

If you are having difficulty feeling grateful to God in the context of your suffering, it may be helpful to note that the Bible never tells us to feel grateful.[12] Instead, we are repeatedly told to "be thankful"—in other words, to recognize God's gifts to us—and to "give thanks"—that is, to express to God our response to recognizing God's gifts. Don't worry about not feeling grateful. Focus on recognizing God's gifts and giving God thanks for them. You may be surprised to find these intentional practices help you to feel more grateful to God. One of our study participants was asked why he gave thanks to God even when he wasn't feeling grateful. He responded,

> In my brief time on this earth, I have learned that in these difficult times, where [feeling] gratitude among other things are lacking, is when I feel closer to God, in an odd way. Not closeness in the sense of me feeling close to him via affirmative actions/practices but by feeling God's closeness to me. And while I have not always felt this way,

> learning this has been one of the greatest things to happen in my life and perhaps nothing has done more to bring me closer to God.[13]

If you aren't currently hurting, gratitude can prepare you for times of suffering. You can become better at noticing the big and small things God is doing so you're less likely to miss something important like the nine lepers and other recipients of Jesus' miracles did.

One final caution regarding gratitude: sometimes we compare ourselves to others, noticing what we have that they don't. This is not gratitude. Psychologists call this downward comparison. It has some benefit because it can help us notice good things in our lives. But it is not the same as gratitude and doesn't have its benefits or strengthen our relationship with Christ in the same way. When you become aware of a gift from God, whether through downward comparison or some other means, be sure to thank God for that gift!

LIGHTS IN THE DARKNESS

Every year in July and August, the Perseid meteor shower can be seen in the Northern Hemisphere—by some people. Jason lives in Los Angeles County, where the only visible stars move back and forth as they approach runways! Jason's family had to drive some distance to get far enough away from the city to see the Perseids on a recent trip. The Perseids are tiny bits of ice and rock strewn from the path of Comet Swift-Tuttle at 133,000 miles per hour, burning at 3,000 degrees Fahrenheit as they enter our atmosphere. Light pollution and ordinary sunlight make this spectacle invisible, even though it's happening continuously. When the sun goes down and darkness falls, other lights emerge. God has scattered gifts throughout the unnoticed background of our lives, like the beautiful stars, meteors, comets, and planets always shining in the sky but obscured by sunlight. Sometimes we need darkness to become aware of them and to give thanks.

Christ also shines in our darkness. Like the sun, the light of Christ can dispel the darkness that surrounds us and fill our world with light and life. Even while describing perplexity, persecution, and being struck down, Paul affirmed "an eternal glory that far outweighs them all" (2 Corinthians 4:17). Suffering positions us to connect with Jesus in a special way, a gift for which we can be grateful. Jesus is the gift available to us in suffering. Leslie, one of our participants, expressed this beautifully: "In the depths of my soul, when everything was going wrong, I felt his love. . . . So it was almost as if the cancer—I hate to say it was a gift, because I wouldn't wish it on anybody—but I think that anything in our relationship with God that brings me closer to him, brings me more into his love, is a blessing in my life. Even if it's painful." We can be thankful for the gift of Christ's presence on our hard roads to glory.

FOR REFLECTION OR DISCUSSION

1. Several practices for cultivating gratitude can be used before, during, and after we go through difficult circumstances:
   - ***Keep a gratitude journal.*** On a regular basis, record things for which you're grateful and to whom you are grateful. The items can be very simple or very profound. Consider writing them in the form of a prayer, as you express your gratitude to God.

- ***Three good things.*** At the end of the day, list or record three good things that happened during the day and why they were good. Consider how they are gifts to you from God.
- ***Find ways to share*** your gratitude with others and have them share their gratitude with you. This will broaden the scope of things for which you can be grateful.

2. The chapter mentions that some gifts from suffering are revealed only with time and perspective. Looking back on past struggles, can you identify any such "delayed gifts" in your own life? How might this insight help you in current or future difficulties?
3. The chapter states that suffering can put us in touch with the fundamental reality of our dependence on God. Reflect on how your own experiences of suffering have revealed your limitations and dependence on God. How has this awareness affected your faith?
4. Reflect on the following passages using lectio divina: 2 Corinthians 12:1-10; James 1:2-4; 1 Thessalonians 5:16-19; Psalm 107:1-9, 43; Romans 5:3-5.

FURTHER READING

Robert A. Emmons, *Gratitude Works! A Twenty-One-Day Program for Creating Emotional Prosperity* (Jossey-Bass, 2013).

Cornelius Plantinga, *Gratitude: Why Giving Thanks Is Key to Our Well-Being* (Brazos, 2024.)

David Steindl-Rast, *Gratefulness, the Heart of Prayer: An Approach to Life in Fullness* (Paulist, 1984).

Ann Voskamp, *One Thousand Gifts: A Dare to Live Fully Right Where You Are* (Thomas Nelson, 2011).

TEN

REMEMBERING OUR MORTALITY

I know that when I pass from this life to the next, he'll be there too. So I'm less worried about dying. I was always worried about dying. So, not so worried about that anymore. I'm not looking forward to it but not scared of it.

ERIC, CANCER SURVIVOR

ALICE WAS ANGRY. As she and Liz drank their coffee, Alice told Liz about her experience at the nursing home where her grandmother was slowly dying. In a sense, her grandmother had already been lost to her family, as her Alzheimer's disease had progressed to the point where she no longer recognized anyone. Now she was lying in a coma, waiting for death to end her struggles. But Alice wasn't angry about that. Her grandmother's death was expected. The family had grieved and, in fact, would be somewhat relieved once the long process of dying was over. No, Alice was angry at the nurse who was pressuring Alice's mother to take extraordinary measures to keep Alice's grandmother alive for a few more days. Her mother had declined, but she was now racked with guilt, having been made to feel she must not love her mother if she wasn't willing to authorize medical interventions that would prolong her half-life in a coma for a few more days.

This story illustrates many interrelated facets of our culture's avoidance of death. Like most people, Alice's grandmother was dying in a facility intended to keep death away from everyday life. Instead of dying at home, as generations of humans throughout history have done, she was in a place set apart for that, out of sight, the better to keep death out of mind. In our culture, the sounds, smells, and environment of death are kept at a distance from most people's everyday lives. Also, note how medical technologies were used: not to heal sickness or prolong a fulfilling life, but to keep death away from the living, at least for a few more days. After all, prolonging her life was not going to make any difference to Alice's unconscious grandmother.

Christians succumb to this cultural avoidance of death too. In fact, several studies have found that more religious people tend to use more heroic end-of-life measures.[1] People in these studies expressed a preference for doctors doing everything possible to keep them alive, even if they were going to die in a few days anyway. They chose this option over a plan of care that focused on relieving pain and discomfort. While there are several ways of understanding these results, one troubling interpretation is that we are more afraid of death than non-religious people. Shouldn't believers, of all people, face death with hope and courage, even amid the undeniable difficulty of it all? Is the extension of life the only goal or priority for Christians?

If suffering disrupts our sense of meaning, the possibility of our death does so on a grand scale. In his seminal book *Meanings of Life*, which launched the psychological study of meaning in 1991, prominent psychologist Roy Baumeister devoted a chapter to how death threatens our sense of meaning.[2] This happens in four ways: death undermines the predictability and controllability of our existence, it eliminates the possibility that we can achieve a sense of meaning in the future, it reminds us that our existence and the meaning framework we have constructed will likely be forgotten, and it nullifies the value of our life's achievements. Baumeister captures well the threat to meaning that death brings when we only consider life "under the sun," without an eternal perspective. In a world with no God, where death remains undefeated, death looms like the great unknown and offers no hope.

It's no wonder, then, that the existential threat of death triggers a series of defensive maneuvers to avoid reminders of the end of life. As a culture, we have had some success in keeping death at bay—at least in the sense of intruding on our everyday lives. We are less successful at not dying. Despite the strenuous efforts of some, we are complete failures in this endeavor, as it would appear that everyone dies. Ben Franklin summed it up when he famously observed that nothing in this world is certain but death and taxes. We must learn to live with the reality of death. But how do we live with death? And why would we want to?

Our faith encourages us to confront the reality of death head-on, not to escape it but to find hope and meaning in the face of it. The death and resurrection of Jesus Christ reframes death from a final end to a doorway opening to unending life. Your current circumstances may be forcing you to think of death—your own, or that of a loved one. This is challenging and painful. It may raise anxiety. But facing death provides an opportunity to draw alongside Jesus, to participate in his suffering, and to reap with him the benefits of the hope of the resurrection. Contemplating death need not be a morbid fixation but can be a way to live more fully in the present and to expand your horizons beyond this lifetime.

THE PSYCHOLOGY OF AVOIDING DEATH: TERROR MANAGEMENT THEORY

Liz experienced her diagnosis with cancer—the "Big C"—as an existential threat. Outside of her conscious control, her body reacted with terror, keeping her up an entire night with her body in fight or flight mode, heart pounding, trying to figure out how to escape death. She isn't alone in this. In our first round of interviews with Christians with cancer diagnoses, we noted that most of them experienced "existential emotions"—a profound sense of existential aloneness,[3] emptiness, groundlessness,[4] terror, despair, and grief that can arise in the face of death.[5]

Building on the work of existential philosophers, psychologists Jeff Greenberg, Tom Pyszczynski, and Sheldon Solomon developed what they called "terror management theory" to show how the awareness of death, and attempts to deny death, shape much of our behavior—usually outside of conscious awareness. That is, fear of death drives many of our behaviors without our realizing it. This theory proposes that we unconsciously handle death anxiety in two primary ways. First, we might hold on to a global meaning system—such as a religious, political, or philosophical system—that ties us to something bigger than us that will transcend our own death. Or, second, we live up to the ideals of our global meaning system, which brings with it a sense of significance and worth that helps keep the threat of death at bay.[6]

In the face of reminders of our mortality, these relatively benign ways of dealing with death anxiety can go awry. In several hundred existing studies based on terror management theory, research has shown that reminders of death have caused people to buckle down on these strategies, often going to extremes. Instead of merely holding to global worldviews, people became more rigid, dogmatic, and hostile toward people with differing worldviews. Rather than just living up to their standards, people engaged in reactive self-enhancing behaviors such as risky driving, excessive consumption of alcohol and food, or acquisition of high-status products.[7]

Because they operate largely outside our conscious awareness, these terror management strategies fail to address the underlying reality of death directly. Honest confrontation with our mortality, in contrast, allows us to challenge our fear, expand our meaning-making, and live fully in the present moment while embracing hope for the future.

THE THEOLOGY OF FACING DEATH: YOU ARE CRUCIFIED WITH CHRIST

Jesus Christ, the Son of God, suffered and died on the cross for the sins of humanity as the ultimate expression of God's love and the means by which we can be reconciled to God and receive the gift of eternal life. This is the heart of the Christian faith. But before we can fully appreciate the significance of Christ's death and resurrection, we must first grapple with the reality of death as an enemy. Throughout Scripture, death is portrayed as a consequence of sin and violation of God's original intent for creation (Genesis 2:17; Romans 5:12). As Paul writes in Romans 6:23, "For the wages of sin is death, but the gift of

God is eternal life in Christ Jesus our Lord." Human death intrudes into God's good world and corrupts and destroys the life and relationships that God intended for us.

In this light, Christ's death on the cross gains greater meaning. By willingly suffering the consequences of sin and enduring the penalty of death that we deserved, Christ identified with us in our mortal condition and offered us the hope of redemption (2 Corinthians 5:21). As John Stott said, "Jesus Christ, who being sinless had no need to die, died our death, the death our sins had deserved."[8] Through his death, Christ conquered the power of sin and death and opened the way for us to receive forgiveness and new life.

The Christian understanding of death does not end with the cross. Christ's resurrection provided the ultimate victory over death and the promise of eternal life for those who trust in him (1 Corinthians 15:20-23). As Paul writes in 1 Corinthians 15:54-55,

> When the perishable has been clothed with the imperishable, and the mortal with immortality, then the saying that is written will come true: "Death has been swallowed up in victory."
>
> "Where, O death, is your victory?
> Where, O death, is your sting?"

Not only does Christ's resurrection provide us with hope regarding our future reality, but it also transforms our lives in the present. Through faith in Christ, we are united with him in his death and resurrection, and even now we begin to experience the new life he offers. Paul reminded the Roman Christians, "We were therefore buried with him through baptism into death in order that, just as Christ was raised from the dead through the glory of the Father, we too may live a new life" (Romans 6:4). This new life carries a different perspective on death and suffering. Rather than avoiding or denying the reality of death at all costs, we are empowered to confront it head-on, trusting in the hope of the resurrection and the promise of eternal life. We can see our own sufferings and mortality in light of Christ's death and resurrection, knowing that they are not the final word. Paul writes in 2 Corinthians 4:17-18, "For our light and momentary troubles are achieving for us an eternal glory that far outweighs them all. So we fix our eyes not on what is seen, but on what is unseen, since what is seen is temporary, but what is unseen is eternal."

We don't know much about the "unseen" and "eternal," which makes leaning into Paul's words difficult. The world we live in now is the world that feels real. For better or worse, it is known. We struggle to imagine what comes after. Maybe we unknowingly believe the cultural stereotypes of the afterlife that suggest a boring half-existence with nothing much to do. Accordingly, if a resurrection-shaped life is to bring hope and courage, we need to furnish our imaginations with better conceptions of what our physically resurrected lives will look like!

Christ has defeated death . . . but sometimes that's not our experience. This is where the practice of memento mori helps us implement Paul's recommendation: contemplating our death and beyond so that we might "fix our eyes . . . on what is unseen." This way we end up focusing not just on how to avoid death, but on the life that is ours in the resurrected Christ. We get tastes of that life even now, but one day the fullness of that resurrection life—which will be completely free from all the sadness and fear of death—will be ours in glory.

MEMENTO MORI: THE CONTEMPLATION OF DEATH

Liz has a "conference friend," Jim, whom she sees and catches up with every year at a Christian psychology conference. She attended the first conference after her cancer diagnosis with some trepidation. Since she typically wears her hair long, her very short "haircut" (a misnomer, since there had been no cutting, just growing-in) prompted many comments from people who didn't know she had been in treatment for cancer. But Jim sought her out. He had heard from others of her diagnosis and wanted to share that he, too, had journeyed with his wife through breast cancer. Her treatment had also been successful, although Jim added that shortly after finishing her cancer treatment, she had been diagnosed with another, unrelated terminal illness. Eventually she learned that it was a misdiagnosis and was now doing well.

What a roller coaster ride! Imagining herself in that situation, Liz verbalized how terrible it must be to escape death once only to be confronted with it a second time. With his usual understated humor, Jim responded, "Oh, no. Turns out, once you've faced death once, it's much easier the second time!"

This resonated with Liz's experience. She noticed a subtle change in herself after her year of cancer treatment, which included facing her mortality. Are you familiar with that sick feeling in the pit of your stomach that comes when something in your life threatens your well-being? It might be a failure, a loss, helplessness when a loved one is in trouble, or something else. When you wake up in the middle of the night, you notice it even before remembering the trouble that has come to you. Liz almost never experiences that sensation any more. When she first noticed its absence, she worried she had become desensitized to suffering in the world.

Then she realized that the sick feeling had caused her to avoid suffering in the past. She didn't want to be reminded of it! She would seek out ways to distract herself from that gnawing feeling, which meant her responsiveness to people who suffered was limited by her fear. After her own cancer experience, she was more likely to respond empathically to people who suffered because she wasn't distracted by her need to avoid the pit of fear. The cancer had forced her to confront her mortality, her fear of death, and she had emerged changed for the better.

In light of the psychological reality of death avoidance and the theological significance of Christ's death and resurrection, how can we learn to confront death in a way that is honest, hopeful, and transformative? One answer is through the practice of memento mori, contemplating death, a spiritual discipline that has deep roots in the Judeo-Christian tradition.

Moses prayed, "Teach us to number our days, that we may gain a heart of wisdom" (Psalm 90:12). And Solomon wrote,

> It is better to go to a house of mourning
>   than to go to a house of feasting,
> for death is the destiny of everyone;
>   the living should take this to heart. (Ecclesiastes 7:2)

Though Christians these days don't often practice the contemplation of their own deaths, this was a regular practice in the past.

Memento mori, which in Latin means "remember that you must die," can be traced back to early Christianity. The Rule of Saint Benedict, written in the sixth century to guide the lives of Benedictine monks, instructed them to "have the expectation of death daily before one's eyes."[9] Medieval Christians put skulls and skeletons on their tombs and tombstones, where believers would see them every time they attended church, as reminders to consider death. The Puritans did the same. Even famous Baptist preacher Charles Spurgeon once preached a sermon on memento mori, urging his listeners to vividly picture their own deaths and reflect on their salvation.[10] More recently, theologian Todd Billings encouraged Christians to practice memento mori because remembering our death helps us remember we are not the main character; God is working and there is a much bigger world than just our own.[11] This brings the great gift of fresh perspective.

Though no psychological research exists examining the benefits of contemplating death from a Christian perspective, there has been at least one study conducted within a secular framework. In this study, psychologists compared a subtle reminder of death commonly used in terror management theory studies with a more direct prompt to participants to ponder their death as "an experiential reality rather than as a nebulous, unspecified concept" by imagining a specific scenario in which one's death is imminent.[12] While the subtle reminder produced the defensive reactions noted above in the participants, the more intentional contemplation of death led to less defensive reactions and more thoughtful reflections regarding themselves, the lives they lived, and the importance of others.

When we recognize that our time on earth is short and uncertain, we are more likely to invest in things that have eternal significance, such as our relationship with God, our love for others, and our stewardship of the gifts and resources we have been given. We are also more likely to live with a sense of gratitude and wonder, recognizing each day as a precious gift from God. And we can face death, our own and that of others, with hope and equanimity.

APPROACHING DEATH WELL

A word of warning. The goal of these exercises is to overcome the fear of death in order to view reality rightly, in light of our eternal destiny, and to free ourselves to live this life in light of that future. If you have no fear of death, if instead you are attracted to death or even struggle with suicidal thoughts, the practice of memento mori is not for you. Death is not something to be glorified. Death is still an enemy—a defeated one, but nonetheless an enemy. If you start practicing memento mori and discover that contemplating your own death in detail pulls you in, stop immediately. We urge you instead to throw yourself into practices that involve other people and that allow you to live in this life with gratitude to God for that gift. If you are struggling with the recent or impending death of a loved one, remember that being free of the fear of death does not mean you won't grieve the loss. It does mean you will be able to grieve differently from "the rest of mankind, who have no hope" (1 Thessalonians 4:13).

There are many ways to practice memento mori, which are listed below. But the essence is the same in all: to remember our inevitable death regularly, not out of some morbid fascination or death wish, but in the context of what Christ has done for us, conquering death through his life, death, and resurrection. Karl Barth wrote, "The Christian must remember death, *memento mori*, since this remembrance of death is *memento Domini*, remembrance of the Lord."[13] Intentionally weave your life into its eschatological (that is, future) context, into the hope of the resurrection, instead of keeping it limited to your life's current existence. Memento mori moves from fear to hope, from a life driven by the attempt to deny death to a life freed to live in receiving and giving God's love into eternity.

> "Where, O death, is your victory?
> Where, O death, is your sting?"
>
> The sting of death is sin, and the power of sin is the law. But thanks be to God! He gives us the victory through our Lord Jesus Christ. (1 Corinthians 15:55-57)

FOR REFLECTION OR DISCUSSION

Choose one of the following ways to practice memento mori:

1. Use lectio divina (which emphasizes slow, meditative reading of Scripture) to contemplate passages on Jesus' death and resurrection, passages about our identification with his death and resurrection, or passages about death. Consider these texts: Psalm 39; Psalm 90:1-12; Ecclesiastes 3:1-8; John 11:1-44; Romans 6:3-11; Romans 14:7-9; 1 Corinthians 15:50-58; Philippians 1: 20-24; 1 Thessalonians 4:13-18.
2. Identify with Christ's suffering through the use of visual images. Intentionally think about your death in connection with Christ's death.
3. Pray the daily examen, a practice developed by Ignatius of Loyola in the sixteenth century to be prayed at the end of the day. While there are several versions of it, one form incorporates memento mori:
   - Step one: Become aware of God's presence.
   - Step two: Ask for the Holy Spirit's guidance to help you see the day in the light of God's grace.
   - Step three: Review the day, noting both positive and negative events and bringing them before God in sorrow, repentance, and gratitude.

- Step four: Remember your death. Consider the day in view of your death. Ask God for help in making any needed changes to your life in light of your death.
- Step five: Look forward to tomorrow, anticipating what you might need from God to get through the next day.[14]

FURTHER READING

Henri J. M. Nouwen, *Our Greatest Gift: A Meditation on Dying and Caring* (HarperOne, 1994).

Matt McCullough, *Remember Death: The Surprising Path to Living Hope* (Crossway, 2018).

Timothy Keller, *On Death* (Penguin, 2020).

J. Todd Billings, *The End of the Christian Life: How Embracing Our Mortality Frees Us to Truly Live* (Brazos, 2020).

ELEVEN

WEAVING OUR STORY OF SUFFERING INTO GOD'S STORY

My faith journey has been strengthened by hearing others tell their faith journeys. So I think it's super important to share with others. . . . I don't have to pretend that everything's been great. Or I don't have to pretend that I'm, like, some super Christian. But to be authentic in telling our stories—I think we need more of that.

Graham, cancer survivor

If you want to know a person, listen to their stories. We are our stories! At her family's urging, Liz's mother, who is in her eighties, has been writing down stories about her life. Her journey has not always been easy. She lost her fiancée to a motorcycle accident in her twenties. After marrying Liz's father, she left behind everything she knew in her home country of Argentina to follow her husband to the United States. Since then, she has moved multiple times as the wife of an Army officer. But her stories are about God's goodness, God's faithfulness, the lessons she has learned and desires to pass on to her family, and, above all, her gratitude to God for the life he gave her.

Another of Liz's elderly relatives, someone who has also weathered significant hardships and losses, tells very different kinds of stories. While equally deserving of compassion, this woman often circles back to her disappointments, unmet expectations, and a sense that life has been unfair to her. It's understandable—pain has a way of narrowing our vision. Yet over time, Liz has watched how the stories these two have woven about their lives have shaped them into very different women. One finds herself surrounded by family and friends who seek out her wisdom and warmth, while the other has become increasingly isolated, which only reinforces her sense of being overlooked. Liz is not alone in her observations: most of us have watched people respond in profoundly different ways to their hardships, and the stories they tell themselves (and others) don't merely reflect their history; they shape them in the present. For good or bad, these stories and how we tell them carry power.

Happy and sad, delightful and depressing, our real experiences and the stories that emerge from them shape and reshape our lives. Pretending otherwise just means we're being formed in ways we're not acknowledging. Honoring our stories enables the positive results of the meaning-making process we have talked about in this book to unfold. Telling our stories, especially the hard and painful ones that accompany our suffering, opens up the opportunity for connection and healing. Feeling genuinely listened to can be transformative because we don't just feel heard; we feel known. We feel loved. We are our stories. And sometimes stories can reshape how we navigate present experiences. Our narratives are the end point of our meaning-making process: they represent how we have woven our suffering into our life stories.

STORIES AND THE MEANING-MAKING PROCESS

While we can communicate meaning using truth statements, stories carry meanings that transcend conscious intention—truths that both storyteller and hearer may not yet have words for. When we tell a story, we reveal more than we consciously know; when we hear one, we understand more than was explicitly said. Liz has often had the experience of telling her husband about a troubling experience, insisting "it's no big deal," only to hear herself reveal through the telling how deeply it affected her. Her husband hears the hurt she didn't know she was carrying, while she discovers feelings she hadn't admitted to herself. The power of story to hold meaning is also illustrated by the Old Testament passage in which Nathan confronts David indirectly (2 Samuel 12:1-7) by weaving a story in such a way that it stirs David's affections and awakens his concerns about injustice. Only when David is captured by the story does Nathan turn to him and announce, "You are the man!"

Stories are not meant merely for confrontation, but also for comfort and courage. They provide an opportunity for us to catch a fresh vision or see something anew that we have stopped fully appreciating. For example, simply saying the words "God loves me" is not nearly as powerful as telling a story of how God lovingly made his presence known during a difficult time. Like an iceberg that lies primarily below the surface, the implicit meanings carried by stories steer our lives in ways we may not realize. Our life stories reflect how we have made meaning of our lives. They tie together our past and our present, and they shape how we see our future. These stories are not static; we construct and reconstruct our experiences, revising the plot in order to incorporate new events.

Psychologist Dan McAdams has spent his long professional career studying the stories people tell about their lives, including those with difficult life events, people whose life stories needed to incorporate unwanted intrusions.[1] He discovered that some people had "good" stories, resulting in resolution and greater flourishing, while other people had "bad" stories, characterized by lack of resolution and ongoing distress.

As might be expected, McAdams found that people who were able to develop a positive ending to their stories fared the best, under some specific conditions. Only positive endings that also fully acknowledged the negative impact of the life event led to well-being. Minimizing distress or selectively focusing only on the good parts of the story were not helpful. Only stories that expressed struggle by grappling with the experience and its consequences, and that showed changes resulting from that struggle, resulted in well-being. These changes could be perceived as personal growth, improved relationships, or different perspectives on life. In other words, McAdams found that easy stories are not typically good stories. Good stories acknowledge pain, are open to struggle, and show change and growth through life experiences.

This is something our participants seemed to know intuitively. Grace said, "Any time I've ever taught or talked to people, I always share my experience. I think it's so important to not put on that 'Christian face' that says, 'Oh, I've got it all together, and I'm fine.' I think it's important for us to share that, you know, 'I struggled with anxiety,' and to be real with that, and to share the struggles—I think that's so important."

Good stories are also generative stories.[2] People with good life stories are not so preoccupied with themselves that they can't see and respond to the needs of others. Good stories reflect a giving stance toward others, working toward building better families, neighborhoods, and societies. Generative people give to others through a variety of activities, including parenting, teaching, and mentoring, but also through sharing their creative gifts and various other activities. Generative people take their pain and use it to benefit others.

Good stories may also contain strong elements of acceptance.[3] Age, illness, and disability bring with them limitations and constraints that will not go away. Acceptance of what has come before and cannot be changed is necessary in order not to be held back by regret and despair. Acceptance allows us to come to terms with our life as it is. This acceptance can lead to wisdom, humility, and the flexibility to navigate uncertainty and unpredictability. Acceptance of the ultimate limitation, mortality, may also be an essential element when age or illness brings close the threat of death. Surrender to God is an important part of acceptance and may be a particularly important practice for achieving acceptance. In sum, good stories are redemptive stories. They show good coming out of bad.

Bad stories, in contrast, are stagnant. They may even show the opposite of redemption by allowing a negative life event to ruin or contaminate anything good that came before it.[4] For example, a contamination story may say that all the good coming out of a relationship is ruined by a bad ending to the relationship, or that all the benefits of education are ruined by needing to drop out.

Bad stories are self-preoccupied; there is no room for concern for others. Bad stories lack meaning; lives are experienced as just a succession of unrelated events.

McAdams found that the stories we tell are shaped by the stories that surround us, the stories that are culturally available to us.[5] We put together the events of our lives, but we draw on the themes and frameworks that are provided to us by our community. We tell our own stories, but our stories, knowingly or unknowingly, are influenced by the bigger stories that surround us.

There is one bigger story available to us—the most important and true story that has ever been told—that has the potential to infuse hope into our life stories: the big story of God's work in the world and how our stories fit into that grand narrative.

SHAPED BY THE BIBLICAL STORY

Christianity provides an overarching story that structures and informs our personal stories. This ancient faith consistently points us back to the goodness of creation and forward toward a liberated renewed cosmos. But it also acknowledges that we live in the in-between space that swirls with the complexity of brokenness and pain, promise and hope. Our imaginations become able to inhabit this space when they are shaped by Scripture.

In the middle of the twentieth century, the Swiss theologian Karl Barth passionately urged his readers to enter "the strange new world within the Bible."[6] He reminded them that Scripture isn't primarily a history book or an ethics manual. The Bible's fundamental goal is to open our eyes to God: here we encounter the Father, Son, and Holy Spirit. Centered on Christ, we discover that "he is the redeemer of the groaning creation about us.

The whole Bible authoritatively announces that God must be all in all; and the events of the Bible are the beginning, the glorious beginning of a new world."[7]

We enter this strange new world in order to encounter the living God and begin to see our own experiences differently. Once we see God and the story of redemption, everything looks different. This doesn't mean we see everything through rose-colored glasses, but it does mean we recognize we are not abandoned, that God is present, that we are loved, and that all things will ultimately be made right. A healthy Christian perspective through suffering will be deeply shaped by this biblical story, the overarching storyline we encounter in the Bible.

Various Christian traditions have tried to capture the grand biblical narrative with these terms: creation, fall, redemption, and consummation. The story goes like this. God creates everything that is not God, and he calls it all "good" (Genesis 1). Genesis opens with human flourishing—humans were meant to delight in God, honor God's creation, and live in harmony with other humans in an effort to reflect God and grow his creation in good and life-giving ways (Genesis 1:28; 2:15).

But all too quickly the narrative shifts from an emphasis on the good of shalom (Genesis 2:25) to a fallen world infiltrated by deceit, death, and disharmony. We are introduced to a voice of temptation and lies (Genesis 3:1-4), to shame and the undermining of relationships (Genesis 3:8-12); bodies are now associated with the pain of childbirth and with suffering that culminates in human death (Genesis 2:16-17; 3:16). Creation is now presented as compromised and distorted in various ways. The goodness of creation continues, but every aspect of it has been touched by the brokenness of sin, death, and the devil.

Thankfully, the story doesn't end with the fall. We now find ourselves also living in a world being redeemed by Jesus of Nazareth. In his life, death, resurrection, and ascended reign, we discover the embodiment of God's compassion for his people. In Christ, we see God's refusal to let the fall be the last word over humanity. Through Jesus' life and death, we discover God's solidarity with us, made most clear by his willingness to face judgment and the darkness of the grave on our behalf. Through Jesus' bodily resurrection and ascension, we can be confident that our current experiences of pain, suffering, and even death will not be the last word.

We don't use the word *consummation* much in our day, except maybe with jokes about "consummating a marriage." But that imagery is relevant, since the last book in the Bible, John's Revelation, portrays humanity's future hope in Christ in terms of a great wedding feast and celebration when Jesus returns. This future day is what the ancient prophets anticipated and longed for. Their vision of the future included the promise that death will be swallowed up, tears wiped away, mourning ended, God's people fully and finally rescued, with joy and gladness exploding.[8]

Allowing these four parts of the story—creation, fall, redemption, consummation—to shape our imaginations can reorient us and guide our path through suffering.[9] Taken together, they help us avoid picking among the competing dynamics we inevitably encounter. There is space for honoring our bodies, delighting in relationships, and feeling the goodness of how God made his world (creation), but there is also encouragement to avoid a spiritually shallow narration of our hurts since Scripture includes space for darkness, deep sadness, and aching lament (fall). In addition, we can maintain some level of confidence even as we currently swim in the waters of uncertainties and affliction (redemption), and we are invited to cultivate biblical hope rather than naive optimism (consummation).

These four parts of the story of redemption remind us where we are currently situated: between redemption and consummation. Oscar Cullman was a Lutheran theologian who lived through World War II. He suggested that the events of the war could help us understand our situation as followers of Jesus Christ.[10] D-Day marked the decisive day when the allied troops successfully stormed the Normandy coast and began to push out the German army. Their accomplishment that day was the beginning of the end; the final victory of the allies over Germany was decided that day. But it wasn't until almost a year later that final victory was declared on V-Day. For the soldiers on the ground, the POWs in camps across Europe, and the waiting families back home, D-Day was an incredible day. It gave hope, and with it, renewed vigor in the fight. Yet there were still many months of hardship and many more casualties of the war before the final victory was achieved. Some of the bloodiest periods of the war occurred during those long months between D-Day and V-Day.

Cullman suggested that we find ourselves in a similar situation: "That event on the cross, together with the resurrection which followed, was the already concluded decisive battle."[11] D-Day has already occurred. The victory is assured. Christ has already won the victory. As Colossians 2:15 puts it, "Having disarmed the powers and authorities, he made a public spectacle of them, triumphing over them by the cross." But it is only the beginning of the end. The cease-fire is still in the future. V-Day, when Jesus will return, is still to come.

Still, in the already-but-not-yet, while we are no longer separated by our sin, we still experience our relationship with God imperfectly. As 1 Corinthians 13:12 picturesquely puts it, "Now we see only a reflection as in a mirror; then we shall see face to face. Now I know in part; then I shall know fully, even as I am fully known." And while sin no longer has the hold on us it once had, we are still "work[ing] out our salvation" while God simultaneously "works in [us] to will and to act in order to fulfill his good purpose" (Philippians 2:12-13). The rest of the effects of sin on the world around us, the suffering, pain, and ugliness, are still there and cling to us. Throughout the New Testament, we are encouraged to look forward to, and prepare for, the day when we will be totally free from our bondage to sin, decay, and suffering. In the meantime, we wrestle to understand how God's love fits with suffering. We are not sure how and why good things happen to "bad" people and bad things happen to "good" people. In truth, we are all living in the space of the now and not yet, and we all struggle with not only our own sin but also the brokenness in the world, our communities, and our lives.

We can't get stuck merely in the "already" or only in the "not yet." When we understand where we are in the story, we can effectively fulfill our role in the narrative. We journey through suffering affirming the goodness of creation while also mourning the disruption and hurt of the fall, which brought disorder, tears, and pain to the human experience. Even though "this is not the way it was supposed to be," we confess God's goodness and the ongoing dignity and significance of humanity.[12] Future hope liberates us to be brutally honest about our present experiences, not pretending that heaven is yet on earth. We long and wait for what is to come. "Christ has died, Christ has risen, and Christ will come again."

BEARING WITNESS

In one of our research projects, we interviewed Black women with cancer diagnoses to understand how they drew on their Christian faith in going through their suffering. Having a story and telling that story, their "testimony," was central to getting through cancer treatment. They drew on the hard-earned wisdom and guidance of their churches. Two common words arise during many Sunday services in Black churches across America: *testify* and *witness*. When Christians from other traditions hear the words *testimony* and *witness*, they may think about sharing the Christian faith with a nonbeliever. But the Black church expression is much broader, reflecting a practice of storytelling that highlights both the genuine challenge faced by a person or community and also signs of God's kind provision and presence.[13]

Testimony was a meaning-making practice for these women in that it provided a structure for telling their stories to themselves and others about what God had done in their lives. As difficult as cancer diagnosis and treatment were, these women attributed a purpose to their experience and found this to be a powerful way of making their suffering meaningful. As one woman testified, "I saw what God has done [for] other people. And I said, 'Oh, God has done this.' But I needed my own personal story that I can say, 'That's what God has done or what he did do.' And [the cancer experience] gave me that. I can tell you what God's done for me—not my mom, not my dad, not my sisters, but what he's done for me."[14] Having and sharing their testimonies brought purpose and courage in the face of the challenges of cancer.

The content of these testimonies brought several things into focus. They emphasized the relational experience of God.

Christianity was no mere intellectual decision. It was framed in deeply relational terms: God loved them and was present to them in intimate ways. Second, in light of God's goodness and presence, they were quick to stress gratitude. In what is sometimes known in the Black community as "praise testimony," they aimed for gratitude to fill their minds and find expression in their words from when they rose out of bed to when they rested their heads on the pillow at night. Third, these women highlighted God's promises. They tended to focus on God's promises of healing, his power to strengthen them, and his willingness to be present with them in their pain. This didn't mean they thought their healing would be immediate since they maintained an eternal perspective. But by emphasizing God's promises from Scripture, these believers found solace and courage in the God who would not let them go, had the power to hold them forever, and would be with them.

These aspects of testimony provided the framework for these women to turn their focus from themselves to others, illustrating the generativity found in McAdams' work. A twofold purpose of glorifying God and helping others consistently emerged in their practice of testimony. Sharing their story amplified purpose and helped these believers resist fatalism and despair. The practice of testimony served both to help the sufferer feel seen and heard while also allowing them to point to God's goodness amid hardship. One of our participants said, "I might not be a Bible scholar, but I sure do have something to say that I've experienced to be able to share with somebody!"

Many of the women also described how they were strengthened through hearing the testimonies of those who had come before them, including the testimonies of people in the Bible. One woman commented, "I saw how God really uses people who have been through something . . . because then they had enough confidence to say, 'God got me out of the lion's den.'" Others mentioned hearing the testimonies of people in their communities who had gone through challenges and were encouraged by how God had acted in their lives.

GOD'S STORY AND OUR SUFFERING

In this book we have attempted to share some of the lessons we have learned about suffering well. The journey through suffering, while unwanted, can be the road to flourishing—the hard road to glory. Sometimes there is no path around the storm; you must instead go right through it. But thankfully, the storm is not the only reality we must keep in mind. We must also lift our gaze and be reminded of the God who is with us in the storm. The central message about suffering in the Christian tradition is that God is redeeming our suffering. But we are not meant to be passive. We have choices to make in how we think about suffering, in how we orient our lives, and in how we engage in the meaning-making practices of our faith. We choose how to shape our stories.

While suffering can feel isolating, we are not alone in our suffering. In these pages, we have attempted to draw alongside you, pointing out the contours of the meanings God provides for our suffering. How we think about our suffering matters. How we situate our suffering in God's larger story matters. We have also provided some practical tools to help you make meaning, putting together the pieces of your story. While some of these practices are better known than others, all of them have their roots in Scripture and have been developed over the centuries by

God's people as concrete spiritual practices to more fully weave their stories into God's story.

We end with a quote from the late Tim Keller, who faced his last journey through pancreatic cancer practicing what he preached. This quote beautifully highlights the uniqueness of the Christian meaning-making framework, and the centrality of God's love in the Christian story:

> Christianity teaches that, contra fatalism, suffering is overwhelming; contra Buddhism, suffering is real; contra karma, suffering is often unfair; but contra secularism, suffering is meaningful. There is a purpose to it, and if faced rightly, it can drive us like a nail deep into the love of God.[15]

Our hope is that, in company with God's people who have walked through pain and suffering before us, you may grow in the capacity to grasp how wide and long and high and deep is God's love in Christ for you. God bless you on your journey.

FOR REFLECTION OR DISCUSSION

1. Reflect on your own life story. When you tell your story, what parts are emphasized? Which are neglected? How have you incorporated experiences of suffering into your narrative? Are there aspects of your story you might reframe in light of this chapter's discussion on "good" and "bad" stories? What connections do you see between the way you tell your story, how you view your life, and the kind of person you are?
2. The chapter discusses the importance of the biblical narrative in shaping our understanding of our own stories. How does viewing your life through the lens of creation, fall, redemption, and consummation change your perspective on

your experiences of suffering? How does God fit into your story? (Or, better, how do you fit into God's story?)

3. Consider the concept of living in the already-but-not-yet between Christ's first and second coming. How does this tension manifest in your own life and struggles? How might it offer both comfort and challenge? How are God's promises and eschatological hope shaping your view of the future?
4. Reflect on the following passages using lectio divina: Psalm 107:1-9; Luke 24:13-35; 2 Corinthians 1:3-7; Hebrews 12:1-3.

FURTHER READING

Craig G. Bartholomew and Michael W. Goheen, *The Drama of Scripture: Finding Our Place in the Biblical Story*, 3rd ed. (Baker Academic, 2024).

Frederick Buechner, *Telling Secrets* (HarperOne, 2000).

Frederick Buechner, *The Sacred Journey: A Memoir of Early Days* (HarperOne, 1991).

ACKNOWLEDGMENTS

While the three of us have our names on the title page, the content of this book owes so much to the various members of the research team who have each brought their strengths to the work we have done together over many years. Crystal Park, whose theory on meaning-making provided the framework for the book, brought a calm and encouraging presence, especially when things didn't go as planned in our empirical studies. Her experience was often brought to bear in talking Liz off the ledge of despair! Eric Silverman provided the first nudge that got the ball rolling, suggesting to Liz that they apply for a small grant to do some work on suffering together. His continued enthusiasm and conference-running skills have strengthened the scholarly reach of our project. Jamie Aten, popularizer extraordinaire, brought his extensive networks and his knowledge of social media to the table, helping us to disseminate our work where it was most needed. Laura Shannonhouse expanded our work in new directions with her passion for helping refugees. Alexis Abernethy lent her expertise in working with Black churches. Laura Captari swooped in to support writing some of our scholarly articles when time and energy ran low.

We have also been blessed with an abundance of talented and committed former and current students and postdocs from Rosemead School of Psychology and the University of Connecticut who supported our work, tirelessly inputting questionnaires, cleaning datasets, writing up method sections, conducting interviews, coding, running stats, leading groups, etc. A special thanks to Grace Lee, Lindsay Snow, Shane Sacco, Dahee Kim, Nicole Chang, Sarah Lawson, and Matthew Duff.

Our work was generously funded by a number of individuals and organizations. Two anonymous individuals helped launch our first study through a Rosemead Faculty Seed/Bridge Grant. The Council for Christian Colleges and Universities funded a Networking Grant that allowed us to expand that original work. While the opinions expressed in this book are those of the authors and do not necessarily reflect the views of the John Templeton Foundation, this book was made largely possible through the support of a generous grant from the John Templeton Foundation which sustained our work through the years. Nick Gibson at JTF provided encouragement as well as valuable guidance on developing measures. Furthermore, an anonymous family foundation, together with the Templeton World Charity Foundation, funded our first foray into the application of work to help suffering Christians; this first project on program development focused on lament.

At InterVarsity Press, we are grateful for the enthusiasm and guidance brought to our project by our editor, Cindy Bunch. She was willing to take a chance on an unusual project, coauthored by three people. Yet she was kind and encouraging, seeing how scholars who had worked together for years from different disciplines could yield some fresh insights—we are so thankful for your supportive vision.

While many helpful individuals have greatly assisted us along the way, a number of people served as "test readers" as we worked to complete the manuscript. All of the following read some of the chapters, but most of them went through the entire book, providing invaluable feedback along the way: Lisa Allen, Jodi and Eric Blick, Arnaldo Cavazos, Charity Chaney, Aly Davis, Christy Grauley, James Hampson, Leah Jones, Jan Leong, Amy Rathburn, and John Yates. We are deeply in their debt. The Office of Academic Research did much of the administrative work for our studies; a special thanks to Shannon Maxwell and Rae Smith.

Several individuals facilitated our access to sources for our qualitative participants; you know who you are! Thank you. Finally, we want to thank the many, many people who gave generously of their time and experiences to participate in our studies. We hope that wading through our many questions to provide us with information was also valuable to you in continuing to process your suffering before God.

Beyond these collective thanks, we each also wanted to briefly offer particular thanks to the following:

Liz Hall: Writing this book has brought back many memories of my own struggles during my year in treatment with cancer. That year marked the beginning of the journey that led to this book. I am so grateful for my church community, Redemption Hill, and the Household of Faith adult class in particular, for the many ways in which they provided practical and spiritual support, in general and especially during that long year of treatment. My work community, Rosemead School of Psychology, made work-life balance easy. The ladies in my book club—Noelle Collins, Kristin Joy Jauregui, Cheri Sandoval, Nancy Marriott—planted flowers in my front yard after dark so I would be surprised by them the next morning, put together a quilt to comfort me (bloodstains and all, Cheri!), and often made me laugh. Laughter really is great medicine! Noelle, you let me share my craziest fears with you without judging me. Thank you. My mom and dad, Rosa and Phil Lewis, brought words from God to calm my fears. My mother stepped in as a substitute mom and caregiver to take care of so many of the tasks of parenting and daily living during that year, and drove me to each of my chemo appointments. My sons, Brennan and Aiden, brought joy and laughter in a hard season. Finally, many thanks to my husband, Todd, who listened patiently to my processing, wasn't afraid of my tears, and took abundant time to simply be there. I have learned so much from all of you about how to walk through suffering.

Thanks also to Dr. Chip Dickens for putting my name forward and to Dr. Mark Yarbrough for inviting me to deliver the W. H. Griffith Thomas Memorial Lectures at Dallas Theological Seminary in 2021. These lectures provided the first context for pulling different projects together into a meaningful whole, and the response encouraged me to consider that our material could really be helpful to Christians going through difficult times. Kelly and Jason, I couldn't ask for better coauthors and look forward to continuing our collaboration!

Kelly M. Kapic: What a joy and honor to work with the whole Templeton team for many years now; I'm especially grateful for Liz and Jason—you two are not just excellent scholars and diligent workers, but you have also become dear friends. The ability to quickly move back and forth between deep laughter and rigorous work is rare, but with you two, it was natural and invigorating.

Many of those who have proved invaluably supportive of me during this research are named above in the group section, but here I would like to add the following individuals, only wishing I could explain specifics about why I so appreciate each of you: Jay and Beth Anne Green, Jeffrey and Betsy Morton, Everett and Stephanie Pierce, Tom Schwanda, Ty Kesier, Brian Fikkert, Chuck DeGroat, Scott Jones, Hans Madueme, Clift Ward,

Emmie Thompson, Herb Ward, Luke Irwin, Jeff Dryden, Jim and Martha Seneff, Norris† and Billie Little, Jeff and Lynn Hall, Brad and Kelli Voyles, Collin and Elizabeth Messer. Additionally, Lookout Mountain Presbyterian Church and Covenant College have been incredibly supportive communities, often serving as the testing ground for much of my wrestling through the topic of suffering. Thanks for allowing me the space to do just that.

While some aspects of our family's journey with suffering are in print, most are not, and only our closest friends (many noted above) and family know how long and hard the pilgrimage has been. Special thanks, therefore, to our family who have consistently prayed for us, offered words of grace and courage, and just supported us through these many years: Gary and Linda Kapic, John and Lynne Malley, Danny and Emily Kapic, David and Jennifer Kapic, Ming and Jennifer Chiou, and Juliette Kapic. But no one knows as well as you, our children, Jonathan and Margot: from childhood to now adulthood, you have been brave, patient (truly *long*-suffering!), gracious, and incredibly kind to me and your mom as you have walked through the years with us. This has been your journey too. We are stunned by your love, forgiveness, humility, and support. Finally, Tabitha. Amid what seems to be the endless journey of suffering, thank you for never settling for plastic Christianity, but instead helping me and many others learn to be more honest about the realities of pain, even as you encourage us to also learn to be more honest about God's goodness amid such hard seasons. Your life brings so much light to this world.

Jason McMartin: I'm grateful for the collegial, warm, and energizing environment provided by Biola University. I have excellent colleagues, among whom Tim Pickavance always provides a ready ear and sage advice. I'm thankful to my deans at

Biola who supported my work with a research leave: Scott Rae, Doug Huffman, Doug Geringer, Ed Stetzer, Doug Daugherty, and Joe De Luna, and to Janelle Aijian and Dave Merrill who covered classes for me.

Friends from Maple Evangelical Church and Granada Heights Friends Church taught me a great deal about how to approach suffering. Participants at academic and non-academic presentations asked probing questions that sharpened my thinking and helped me see that we potentially had something useful to share with the Church.

My coauthors, Liz and Kelly, are delightful and encouraging collaborators and friends. I have learned a great deal from each of you and could not have written this book without you. I have been so blessed to work with you and the rest of the research team over these past years. I could not ask for better teammates.

My in-laws Andy and Debbie Pulsipher, and the Pavlovic and Shevlin families asked regularly about this project and have cheered me onwards. Friends from all of our spheres of life have shown interest over several years. I'm grateful to all of you, even though there are too many to name individually.

My sons, Jeremy and Eric, delight me and distract me, in all of the right sorts of ways. The Lord bless you and keep you. I would not have gotten anywhere apart from the sacrifices of my parents, David and Lois, and my wife, Kelly, who helped make my education and career and very life possible. My love to all of you.

I dedicate this book to my dear friends the Crawfords. Scott drew near to Christ in his suffering; I hope this book will help others approximate his nearly inimitable example. May Christ make his home with us and show his kindness to us on our journeys.

APPENDIX

LEADER'S GUIDE FOR GROUP STUDY

This guide is designed to help you lead a group through *When the Journey Hurts: Finding Meaning in Suffering for Heart, Mind, and Soul* over the course of six sessions. The journey through suffering is often lonely, but it need not be walked alone. As we've emphasized throughout the book, we were created for community, and our brothers and sisters in Christ can provide invaluable support as we navigate difficult seasons.

The questions and exercises at the end of the chapters are a good way to prompt discussion in each session. Consider beginning each session with a broader question, such as "What caught your attention in the chapter(s) this week?" If possible, end each session with a minute or two of quiet reflection and then conclude in prayer. Given that the topic of suffering is what centers these discussions, it's helpful to make sure each person is prayed for at the end, as this helps ground the small group and avoids reducing the gathering to abstract ideas. This could be as simple as everyone agreeing to pray for the person on their right or left. However, many find even small groups intimidating to pray in, so it may also be helpful to have people break into pairs in order to share their requests and pray for each other.

Beginning with session four, participants will be introduced to specific meaning-making practices. To maximize the benefit of these practices, this guide includes suggestions for weekly practice intentions that participants can implement between sessions. This approach allows group members to experience these practices firsthand and share their insights with the group in order to increase understanding and encourage each other.

GENERAL GUIDELINES FOR GROUP LEADERS

- ***Create a safe space.*** Participants will be sharing vulnerable experiences. Establish ground rules about confidentiality and respectful listening. Encourage participants to "do to others as you would have them do to you" (Luke 6:31).
- ***Balance structure and flexibility.*** While this guide provides a structure, be sensitive to the needs of your group. Some discussions may need more time than anticipated.
- ***Prepare in advance.*** Familiarize yourself with the chapter content and questions before each meeting.
- ***Practice active listening.*** Model attentive, empathetic listening for your group. Encourage other group members to also support each other in this way. Some find it a powerful gesture to gather phones at the start of the meeting (in a non-legalistic way) in order to minimize distractions and honor the people there, thus encouraging active listening. Everyone picks them up again when the time of prayer is concluded.
- ***Manage participation.*** Encourage everyone to contribute, but respect that some may need time before feeling

comfortable sharing. If someone in the group tends to dominate, respectfully address this outside of the group.

- ***Mind the time.*** Allow sufficient time for both discussion and prayer.
- ***Provide pastoral support.*** Be prepared to recommend professional counseling or pastoral care for group members who may need additional support. Remember that your role is not to have all the answers or to "fix" anyone's suffering.

SIX-SESSION FORMAT

Session 1: Understanding Suffering and Meaning (Chapters 1-2)

Key concepts

- The meaning-making model and how suffering disrupts our global meaning system
- Problems with vague, triumphalist, and defensive theologies of suffering

Session 2: Christian Flourishing and Intimacy with God (Chapter 3)

Key concepts

- Love as the center of Christian flourishing
- The three components of intimacy with God: being present, being close, and abiding
- How suffering can facilitate deeper relationship with God

Session 3: Purpose in Suffering (Chapter 4)

Key concepts

- The distinction between causes and purposes in suffering
- How suffering draws us into deeper friendship with Christ
- How suffering helps us become more like Christ and do the things Christ does

Session 4: Identification and Lament (Chapters 5-6)

Key concepts

- Three ways of identifying with Christ in suffering: partnering with the Spirit, following Christ's example, and intimacy
- The structure and purpose of biblical lament
- How these practices promote meaning-making

Weekly practice intention

At the end of the session, have each participant set a specific intention for practicing identification with Christ or lament during the coming week. For example:

- "I will spend ten minutes each morning meditating on Isaiah 53, connecting Christ's suffering with my current challenges."
- "I will write one brief lament prayer each evening, following the five-part structure."
- "When I feel overwhelmed, I will pause to identify how my suffering connects with Christ's."

Ask participants to note their experiences in a journal and be prepared to share briefly at the next meeting about how the practice affected them.

Session 5: Surrender and Forgiveness (Chapters 7-8)

Key concepts

- Surrender as loving, active, inward yielding to God
- What forgiveness is and is not
- The psychological and spiritual benefits of these practices

Weekly practice intention

At the end of the session, have each participant set a specific intention for practicing surrender or forgiveness during the coming week. For example:

- "I will practice surrendering my daily anxieties by praying the Serenity Prayer each morning and evening."
- "I will work through one step of the REACH forgiveness model this week for a specific hurt I'm struggling to forgive."
- "I will identify one area where I'm trying to control outcomes and practice surrendering it to God daily."

Ask participants to note in a journal how these practices affected their emotional state and relationship with God. Begin the next session by having participants briefly share their experiences.

Session 6: Gratitude, Confronting Mortality, and Testimony (Chapters 9-11)

Key concepts

- Practicing gratitude in the midst of suffering
- Confronting mortality (memento mori) as a Christian practice
- Weaving our stories of suffering into God's larger story

Weekly practice intention

At the end of the session, have each participant set a specific intention for practicing gratitude, memento mori, or testimony during the coming week. For example:

- "I will write down three things I'm grateful for each evening, including during difficult moments."
- "I will spend ten minutes each day reflecting on Psalm 90:12 ('Teach us to number our days') and how awareness of mortality reshapes my priorities."

- "I will identify one aspect of my suffering story and consciously connect it to God's larger story of redemption through journaling or prayer."

Since this is the final session, encourage participants to continue these practices and perhaps meet informally to share how they are integrating these practices into their daily lives.

FINAL THOUGHTS

As you lead your group through this book, remember that the goal is not just intellectual understanding, but Spirit-led transformation. The practices in this book—identifying with Christ, lament, surrender, forgiveness, gratitude, remembering our mortality, and testimony—are meant to be lived out before God and in community.

Consider ways to continue supporting one another in these practices even after the formal study concludes. Perhaps participants might form smaller accountability groups or schedule check-ins to continue sharing how these meaning-making practices are shaping their approach to suffering.

May God bless you and your group as you journey together through the hurts of this life.

NOTES

PREFACE: SUFFERING

[1]For more on how pain is "good," see the reflections of a physician who specialized in leprosy: Paul Brand and Philip Yancey, *The Gift of Pain* (Zondervan, 1993), 3-13.

[2]Laura A. King, "The Hard Road to the Good Life: The Happy, Mature Person," *Journal of Humanistic Psychology* 41, no. 1 (2001): 51-72.

[3]Kelly M. Kapic, *Embodied Hope: A Theological Meditation on Pain and Suffering* (IVP Academic, 2017).

[4]Jeanne M. Slattery and Crystal L. Park, "Meaning Making and Spiritually Oriented Interventions," in *Spiritually Oriented Interventions for Counseling and Psychotherapy*, ed. Jamie D. Aten, Mark R. McMinn, and Everett L. Worthington (American Psychological Association, 2011), 15-40.

1. SUFFERING AND MEANING

[1]Friedrich Wilhelm Nietzsche, *On the Genealogy of Morals*, trans. Douglas Smith, Oxford World's Classics (Oxford University Press, 2009), 136.

[2]Viktor Frankl, *Man's Search for Meaning*, 3rd ed. (Touchstone, 1984), 84.

[3]Crystal L. Park, "Making Sense of the Meaning Literature: An Integrative Review of Meaning Making and Its Effects on Adjustment to Stressful Life Events," *Psychological Bulletin* 136, no. 2 (March 2010): 257-301.

[4]Jeremy D. W. Clifton et al., "Primal World Beliefs," *Psychological Assessment* 31, no. 1 (2019): 82-99.

[5]Eleonore Stump, *Wandering in Darkness: Narrative and the Problem of Suffering* (Clarendon, 2010), 6-13, https://doi.org/10.1037/pas0000639.

[6]Park, "Making Sense of the Meaning Literature."

[7]Lawrence G. Calhoun and R. G. Tedeschi, "The Foundations of Posttraumatic Growth: An Expanded Framework," in *Handbook of Posttraumatic Growth*, ed. L. G. Calhoun and R. G. Tedeschi (Erlbaum, 2006), 3-23. Crystal L. Park et al., "Assessment and Prediction of Stress-Related Growth," *Journal of Personality* 64, no. 1 (1996): 71-105.

[8]Calhoun and Tedeschi, "Foundations of Posttraumatic Growth." Stephen Joseph and P. Alex Linley, "Growth Following Adversity: Theoretical Perspectives and Implications for Clinical Practice," *Clinical Psychology Review* 26 (2006): 1041-53.

[9]Joseph and Linley, "Growth Following Adversity."

[10]Calhoun and Tedeschi, "Foundations of Posttraumatic Growth." Joseph and Linley, "Growth Following Adversity."

[11]Christopher Peterson et al., "Strengths of Character and Posttraumatic Growth," *Journal of Traumatic Stress* 21, no. 2 (2008): 214-17.

[12]Calhoun and Tedeschi, "Foundations of Posttraumatic Growth." Joseph and Linley, "Growth Following Adversity."

[13]M. Elizabeth Lewis Hall, "Psychology and Theodicy: The Meaning-Making Model and Growth," in *T&T Clark Companion to Suffering and the Problem of Evil*, ed. Matthias Grebe and Johannes Grössl (T&T Clark, 2023), n.p.

[14]Claus Westermann, "כבד יקר," *Theological Lexicon of the Old Testament*, 2:593. For more detailed studies, see Carey C. Newman, "Glory, Glorify [בכ דו, kavodh; δόξα doxa, δοξάζω doxazō]," *New Interpreter's Dictionary of the Bible* 2:576–80; Claus Westermann, "דבכ kbd to be heavy," *Theological Lexicon of the Old Testament* 2:590–602; Kittel and von Rad, "δοκέω, δόξα, δοξάζω, συνδοξάζω, ἔνδοξος, ἐνδοξάζω, παράδοξος," *Theological Dictionary of the New Testament*, 2:232–55.

[15]Laura A. King, "The Hard Road to the Good Life: The Happy, Mature Person," *Journal of Humanistic Psychology* 41, no. 1 (2001): 51-72.

2. PROBLEMATIC ROADMAPS

[1]Glenn Pemberton, *Hurting with God: Learning to Lament with the Psalms* (Abilene Christian University Press, 2012).

[2]Julie J. Exline and Eric D. Rose, "Religious and Spiritual Struggles," in *Handbook of the Psychology of Religion and Spirituality*, ed. Raymond F. Paloutzian and Crystal L. Park, 2nd ed. (Guilford, 2013), 380-98.

[3]Jacqueline Ruth Mickley et al., "God and the Search for Meaning Among Hospice Caregivers," *The Hospice Journal* 13, no. 4 (1998): 1-17.

[4]Terry Lynn Gall and Cynthia Bilodeau, "'Why Me?'—Women's Use of Spiritual Causal Attributions in Making Sense of Breast Cancer," *Psychology & Health* 32, no. 6 (2017): 709-27.

[5]Joshua A. Wilt et al., "Theological Beliefs About Suffering and Interactions with the Divine," *Psychology of Religion and Spirituality* 9, no. 2 (2017): 137.

[6]Gall and Bilodeau, "Why Me?"

3. CHOOSING BETTER DESTINATIONS

[1]Roy F. Baumeister et al., "Some Key Differences Between a Happy Life and a Meaningful Life," *Journal of Positive Psychology* 8, no. 6 (2013): 505-16, http://dx.doi.org/10.1080/17439760.2013.830764.

[2]C. S. Lewis, *The Problem of Pain* (HarperSanFrancisco, [1940] 1996), 106-7.

[3]Mary C. Daly et al., "Dark Contrasts: The Paradox of High Rates of Suicide in Happy Places," *Journal of Economic Behavior & Organization* 80, no. 3 (2011): 435-42. According to https://ourworldindata.org/happiness-and-life-satisfaction, *life satisfaction* is measured by the "Cantril Ladder," in which participants are instructed, "Please imagine a ladder, with steps numbered from 0 at the bottom to 10 at the top. The top of the ladder represents the best possible life for you, and the bottom of the ladder represents the worst possible life for you. On which step of the ladder would you say you personally feel you stand at this time?"

[4]For more on this argument and a distinctly Christian account of human flourishing, see Brian Fikkert and Kelly M. Kapic, *Becoming Whole: Why the Opposite of Poverty isn't the American Dream* (Moody Publishers, 2019).

[5]For more on the theological and psychological background of this claim, see Kelly M. Kapic et al., "A Theology of Human Flourishing for Positive Psychology Pedagogy," *Journal of Psychology and Christianity* 42, no. 1 (2023): 4-14.

[6]Raymond Canning, *The Unity of Love for God and Neighbour in St. Augustine* (Augustinian Historical Institute, 1993). Rowan Williams, *On Augustine* (Bloomsbury, 2016).

[7]For a fuller unpacking of how the triune love of God is received, participated in, and extended to others, see Kelly M. Kapic, *Christian Life*, in New Studies in Dogmatics (Zondervan, 2025), chap. 2.

[8]C. S. Lewis, *The Last Battle* (HarperTrophy, 2000).

[9]Edward Dutton et al., "The Myth of the Stupid Believer: The Negative Religiousness-IQ Nexus Is Not on General Intelligence (g) and Is Likely a Product of the Relations Between IQ and Autism Spectrum Traits," *Journal of Religion and Health* 59, no. 3 (2019): 1567-79, https://doi.org/10.1007/s10943-019-00926-3; Edward Dutton et al., "The Mutant Says in His Heart, 'There Is No God': The Rejection of Collective Religiosity Centered Around the Worship of Moral Gods Is Associated with High Mutational Load," *Evolutionary Psychological Science* 4 (2018): 233-44; Catherine Caldwell-Harris et al., "Religious Belief Systems of Persons with High Functioning Autism," Proceedings of the 33rd Annual Meeting of the Cognitive Science Society (2011): 3362-66, http://csjarchive.cogsci.rpi.edu/proceedings/2011/papers/0782/paper0782.pdf; Ara

Norenzayan et al., "Mentalizing Deficits Constrain Belief in a Personal God.," PLOS ONE 7, no. 5 (2012): artIDe36880, http://journals.plos.org/plosone/article?id=10.1371/journal.pone.0036880.

[10]See, for example, J. I. Packer, "The 'Wretched Man' Revisited: Another Look at Romans 7:14-25," in *Romans and the People of God: Essays in Honor of Gordon D. Fee on the Occasion of His 65th Birthday*, ed. Sven K. Soderlund and N. T. Wright (Eerdmans, 1999), 70-81.

[11]Kate Bowler, *Everything Happens for a Reason: And Other Lies I've Loved* (SPCK, 2019), 121-22.

[12]Brother Lawrence, *The Practice of the Presence of God: The Best Rule of Holy Life* (Delhi Open Books, 2020), 11th letter.

[13]William Ickes et al., "Closeness as Intersubjectivity: Social Absorption and Social Individuation," in *Handbook of Closeness and Intimacy*, ed. Debra Mashek and Arthur Aron (Lawrence Erlbaum, 2004), 357-74.

[14]Arthur Aron et al., "Closeness as Including Other in the Self," in *Handbook of Closeness*, 27242.

[15]Eleonore Stump, *Atonement* (Oxford University Press, 2018), 139.

[16]Nicholas J. S. Gibson, "The Experimental Investigation of Religious Cognition" (doctoral diss., University of Cambridge, 2006); Sara D. Hodges et al., "Nearer My God to Thee: Self-God Overlap and Believers' Relationships with God," *Self and Identity* 12, no. 3 (2013): 337-56, https://doi.org/10.1080/15298868.2012.674212.

[17]Arthur Aron and Elaine N. Aron, "Self-Expansion Motivation and Including Other in the Self," in *Handbook of Personal Relationships: Theory, Research and Interventions,* 2nd ed., ed. Steve Duck (Wiley, 1997), 251-70; Arthur Aron et al., "Inclusion of Other in the Self Scale and the Structure of Interpersonal Closeness," *Journal of Personality and Social Psychology* 63, no. 4 (1992): 596-612, https://doi.org/10.1037/0022-3514.63.4.596.

[18]Arthur Aron et al., "Falling in Love: Prospective Studies of Self-Concept Change," *Journal of Personality and Social Psychology* 69, no. 6 (1995): 1102-12.

[19]J. Todd Billings, *Union with Christ: Reframing Theology and Ministry for the Church* (Baker Academic, 2011), 35-61.

[20]Kristin D. Neff, "Self-Compassion: Theory, Method, Research, and Intervention," *Annual Review of Psychology* 74 (2023): 193-218.

[21]Philip R. Shaver et al., "Attachment Security as a Foundation for Kindness Toward Self and Others," in *Oxford Handbook of Hypo-Egoic Phenomena,* ed. Kirk W. Brown and Mark R. Leary (Oxford University Press, 2017): 223-42.

[22]Javier García-Campayo et al., "Exploring the Relationship Between Self-Compassion and Compassion for Others: The Role of Psychological Distress and Wellbeing," *Assessment* 31, no. 5 (2023): 1038-51.

[23]Kristin D. Neff, "Self-Compassion."

[24]Adapted from Robert A. Emmons, *The Psychology of Ultimate Concerns: Motivation and Spirituality in Personality* (Guilford Press, 1999).

[25]C. S. Lewis, *The Four Loves* (Harcourt, Brace & World, 1960), 169-70.

4. PURPOSES FOR SUFFERING

[1]C. S. Lewis, *Till We Have Faces: A Myth Retold* (Collins, Fount Paperbacks, 1980).

[2]Lewis, *Till We Have Faces*, 305.

[3]M. Elizabeth Lewis Hall et al., "The Varieties of Redemptive Experiences: A Qualitative Study of Meaning-Making in Evangelical Christian Cancer Patients," *Psychology of Religion and Spirituality* 12, no. 1 (2020): 13-25.

[4]Eleonore Stump, *Wandering in Darkness: Narrative and the Problem of Suffering* (Oxford University Press, 2010), 124-28. The effects of other people's sins can also leave us fragmented, sometimes with a sense of shame even when we are not personally "guilty" of doing wrong.

[5]Stacey E. McElroy-Heltzel et al., "The Role of Spiritual Fortitude and Positive Religious Coping in Meaning in Life and Spiritual Well-Being Following Hurricane Matthew," *Journal of Psychology and Christianity* 37, no. 1 (2018): 17-27.

5. IDENTIFYING WITH CHRIST'S SUFFERING

[1]Constantine R. Campbell, *Paul and Union with Christ: An Exegetical and Theological Study* (Zondervan, 2012).

[2]M. Elizabeth Lewis Hall et al., "The Christian Sanctification of Suffering Scale: Measure Development and Relationship to Well-Being," *Mental Health, Religion & Culture* 24, no. 8 (2021): 796-813, https://doi.org/10.1080/13674676.2021.1884670.

[3]Neal Krause and Elena Bastida, "Religion, Suffering, and Health among Older Mexican Americans," *Journal of Aging Studies* 23, no. 2 (2009): 114-23, https://doi.org/10.1016/j.jaging.2008.11.002.

[4]M. Elizabeth Lewis Hall, "Suffering as Formation: The Hard Road to Glory," in *The Holy Spirit and Christian Formation: Multidisciplinary Perspectives*, ed. Diane J. Chandler (Palgrave Macmillan, 2016), 69-88.

[5]Rosemary De Castella and Janette Graetz Simmonds, "'There's a Deeper Level of Meaning as to What Suffering's All About': Experiences of Religious and

Spiritual Growth Following Trauma," *Mental Health, Religion & Culture* 16, no. 5 (2013): 536-56, https://doi.org/10.1080/13674676.2012.702738.

[6]Michael J. Gorman, *Cruciformity: Paul's Narrative Spirituality of the Cross* (Eerdmans, 2001), 329.

[7]Eleonore Stump, *Wandering in Darkness: Narrative and the Problem of Suffering* (Clarendon, 2010).

[8]Krause and Bastida, "Religion, Suffering, and Health."

[9]De Castella and Graetz Simmonds, "'There's a Deeper Level.'"

[10]Rachel Sing-Kiat Ting and Terri Watson, "Is Suffering Good? An Explorative Study on the Religious Persecution among Chinese Pastors," *Journal of Psychology and Theology* 35, no. 3 (2007): 202-10, https://doi.org/10.1177/009164710703500303.

[11]M. Elizabeth Lewis Hall et al., "Suffering with Christ: Emic Christian Coping and Relation to Well-Being," *SSM–Mental Health* 2 (December 2022): 100158.

[12]Sammie Lee et al., "When Does Identifying With Christ's Suffering Help? A Moderated Moderation Analysis," *Journal of Psychology and Theology* 53, no. 3 (2025); 259-74, https://doi.org/10.1177/00916471251324603.

[13]Malcolm Guite, "XII Jesus Dies on the Cross," ©Malcolm Guite. Published in *Sounding the Seasons: Seventy Sonnets for the Church Year* (Canterbury, 2012), 43, used by permission, permissions@hymnsam.co.uk.

6. LAMENT

[1]Glenn Pemberton, *Hurting with God: Learning to Lament with the Psalms* (Abilene Christian University Press, 2012), 39.

[2]Michael J. Rhodes, "Why Don't We Sing Justice Songs in Worship?" *Christianity Today*, Sept 30, 2021, www.christianitytoday.com/2021/09/rhodes-ccli-top-25-worship-songs-singing-justice-songs.

[3]For an accessible volume focused on helping Christians become more honest in prayer, see Kyle Strobel and John Coe, *Where Prayer Becomes Real: How Honesty with God Transforms Your Soul* (Baker, 2021).

[4]Lawrence G. Calhoun and Richard G. Tedeschi, "The Foundations of Posttraumatic Growth: An Expanded Framework," in *Handbook of Posttraumatic Growth*, ed. Lawrence G. Calhoun and Richard G. Tedeschi (Erlbaum, 2006), 3-23.

[5]Jeanne M. Slattery and Crystal L. Park, "Meaning Making and Spiritually Oriented Interventions," in *Spiritually Oriented Interventions for Counseling and Psychotherapy*, ed. Jamie D. Aten et al. (American Psychological Association, 2011), 15-40.

[6]David B. Feldman and C. Richard Snyder, "Hope and the Meaningful Life: Theoretical and Empirical Associations Between Goal-Directed Thinking and

Life Meaning," *Journal of Social and Clinical Psychology* 24, no. 3 (2005): 401-21; İlhan Yalçın and Asude Malkoç, "The Relationship Between Meaning in Life and Subjective Well-Being: Forgiveness and Hope as Mediators," *Journal of Happiness Studies* 16, no. 4 (2015): 915-29.

[7]Eugene Peterson, *Answering God: The Psalms as Tools for Prayer* (HarperOne, 1991), 122.

[8]J. Todd Billings, *Rejoicing in Lament: Wrestling with Incurable Cancer and Life in Christ* (Brazos, 2015), 38.

7. SURRENDER

[1]Elisabeth Sifton, *The Serenity Prayer: Faith and Politics in Times of Peace and War* (Norton, 2005), 30.

[2]The first portion of the prayer is widely attributed to Niebuhr (see Sifton, *The Serenity Prayer, 277)*; the remainder of the prayer is contested, and can be found in many popular sources (e.g., Chad Napier, "The Serenity Prayer: 'God grant me the serenity to . . .,'" Christianity.com, May 14, 2025, www.christianity.com/wiki/prayer/what-is-the-serenity-prayer-is-it-biblical.html).

[3]Bill Watterson, "Calvin and Hobbes by Bill Watterson for August 28, 1992," *GoComics*, accessed October 10, 2021.

[4]M. Elizabeth Lewis Hall et al., "Spiritual Surrender: Initial Appraisals of Cancer Diagnoses in Black Christian Women," *Journal of Black Psychology* 50, no. 3 (2024): 365-87, https://doi.org/ 10.1177/00957984241232942.

[5]Laura Shannonhouse et al., "Spiritual Surrender: Measurement of an Emic Christian Religious Coping Strategy," *Spirituality in Clinical Practice* 11, no. 2 (2024): 173-85, https://doi.org/10.1037/scp0000314.

[6]M. Elizabeth Lewis Hall et al., "Theodicy or Not?: Spiritual Struggles of Evangelical Cancer Survivors," *Journal of Psychology and Theology* 47, no. 4 (2019): 259-77, https://doi.org/10.1177/0091647118807187.

[7]Hall et al., "Spiritual Surrender."

[8]Jean Baptiste Saint-Jure and Claude de la Colombiere, *Trustful Surrender to Divine Providence: The Secret of Peace and Happiness* (TAN Books, 1984).

[9]Peter C. Hill et al., "Glad Intellectual Dependence on God: A Theistic Account of Intellectual Humility," *Journal of Psychology and Christianity* 37, no. 3 (Fall 2018): 198.

[10]Jamie Aten, *A Walking Disaster: What Surviving Katrina and Cancer Taught Me About Faith and Resilience* (Templeton, 2020).

[11]Aten, *Walking Disaster,* loc 1560.

[12]C. S. Lewis, *The Problem of Pain* (New York: HarperCollins, 2001), 88-89.

8. FORGIVENESS

[1]Xiao Chen et al., "Turn the Other Cheek vs. A Tooth: The Reducing Effects of Forgiveness and Revenge on Anger," *Acta Psychologica Sinica* 49 (2017): 241-53; Renate Ysseldyk et al., "Revenge Is Sour, but Is Forgiveness Sweet? Psychological Health and Cortisol Reactivity among Women with Experiences of Abuse," *Journal of Health Psychology* 24, no. 14 (2019): 2003-21; Michael E. McCullough et al., "Vengefulness: Relationships with Forgiveness, Rumination, Well-Being, and the Big Five," *Personality and Social Psychology Bulletin* 27, no. 5 (2001): 601-10, https://doi. org/10.1177/0146167201275008.

[2]Lewis B. Smedes, *Forgive and Forget: Healing the Hurts We Don't Deserve* (Harper & Row, 1984).

[3]Liz heard Dr. Worthington state this at a talk given at the Christian Association for Psychological Studies International Convention, April 2012, in Washington, D. C.

[4]Feng Gao et al., "Forgiveness and Subjective Well-Being: A Meta-Analysis Review," *Personality and Individual Differences* 186 (2022): 111350, https://doi .org/10.1016/j.paid.2021.111350.

[5]Yu-Rim Lee and Robert D. Enright, "A Meta-Analysis of the Association Between Forgiveness of Others and Physical Health," *Psychology & Health* 34, no. 5 (2019): 626-43, https://doi.org/10.1080/08870446.2018.1554185. Kyler R. Rasmussen et al., "Meta-Analytic Connections Between Forgiveness and Health: The Moderating Effects of Forgiveness-Related Distinctions," *Psychology & Health* 34, no. 5 (2019): 515-34, https://doi.org/10.1080/08870446.2018.1545906.

[6]Naomi Takada and Ken-ichi Ohbuchi, "True and Hollow Forgiveness, Forgiveness Motives, and Conflict Resolution," *International Journal of Conflict Management* 24, no. 2 (2013): 184-200, https://doi.org/ 10.1108/10444061311316799.

[7]Mickie L. Fisher and Julie Juola Exline, "Self-Forgiveness Versus Excusing: The Roles of Remorse, Effort, and Acceptance of Responsibility," *Self and Identity* 5, no. 2 (2006): 127-46.

[8]Don E. Davis et al., "Forgiving the Self and Physical and Mental Health Correlates: A Meta-Analytic Review," *Journal of Counseling Psychology* 62, no. 2 (2015): 329-35, http://dx.doi.org/10.1037/cou0000063.

[9]Everett L. Worthington Jr., *Steps to REACH Forgiveness and to Reconcile* (Pearson Learning Solutions, 2008).

9. GRATITUDE

[1]Corrie Ten Boom, Elizabeth Sherrill, and John Sherrill, *The Hiding Place*, 35th anniv. ed. (Chosen Books, 2006), 209-10. The entire scene is worth reading, including just two pages earlier, when Betsie and Corrie find a new way to

identify with Christ and to thank him when their clothes are taken from them at their arrival.

[2]Kelly M. Kapic, *The God Who Gives: How the Trinity Shapes the Christian Story* (Zondervan, 2018).

[3]Kate Bowler, *Everything Happens for a Reason: And Other Lies I've Loved* (Random House, 2018), 120-22.

[4]C. S. Lewis, *The Problem of Pain* (Collier, 1962), 90. Kelly M. Kapic, *You're Only Human: How Your Limits Reflect God's Design and Why That's Good News* (Brazos, 2022).

[5]David Steindl-Rast, *Gratefulness, the Heart of Prayer: An Approach to Life in Fullness* (Paulist, 1984).

[6]Barbara L. Fredrickson, "The Role of Positive Emotions in Positive Psychology: The Broaden-and-Build Theory of Positive Emotions," *American Psychologist* 56, no. 3 (2001): 218-26.

[7]Barbara L. Fredrickson, "Gratitude, Like Other Positive Emotions, Broadens and Builds," *The Psychology of Gratitude* 145 (2004): 145-66.

[8]Chih-Che Lin, "Impact of Gratitude on Resource Development and Emotional Well-Being," *Social Behavior and Personality* 43, no. 3 (2015): 493-504; Alex M. Wood et al., "Gratitude and Well-Being: A Review and Theoretical Integration," *Clinical Psychology Review* 30, no. 7 (2010): 890-905.

[9]Alex M. Wood et al., "The Role of Gratitude in the Development of Social Support, Stress, and Depression: Two Longitudinal Studies," *Journal of Research in Personality* 42, no. 4 (2008): 854-71.

[10]Barbara L. Fredrickson and Thomas Joiner, "Positive Emotions Trigger Upward Spirals Toward Emotional Well-Being," *Psychological Science* 13, no. 2 (2002): 172-75.

[11]Kelly Yu-Hsin Liao and Chih-Yuan Weng, "Gratefulness and Subjective Well-being: Social Connectedness and Presence of Meaning as Mediators," *Journal of Counseling Psychology* 65, no. 3 (2018): 383-93.

[12]Kent Dunnington, "Being Grateful and Feeling Grateful: Reconsidering the Phenomenology of Gratitude to God," *The Journal of Positive Psychology* 19, no. 1 (2024): 1-10, https://doi.org/10.1080/17439760.2023.2179937.

[13]M. Elizabeth Lewis Hall et al., "Gratitude to God: Distinguishing between Affect and Cognition," *Journal of Psychology and Christianity* 43, no. 3 (2024): 246-63.

10. REMEMBERING OUR MORTALITY

[1]Tracy A. Balboni et al., "Religiousness and Spiritual Support Among Advanced Cancer Patients and Associations with End-of-Life Treatment Preferences and

Quality of Life," *Journal of Clinical Oncology* 25, no. 5 (2007): 555-60; Gala True et al., "Treatment Preferences and Advance Care Planning at End of Life: The Role of Ethnicity and Spiritual Coping in Cancer Patients," *Annals of Behavioral Medicine* 30, no. 2 (2005):174-79; Andrea C. Phelps et al., "Religious Coping and Use of Intensive Life-Prolonging Care Near Death in Patients With Advanced Cancer," *Journal of the American Medical Association* 30, no. 11 (2009): 1140-47.

[2]Roy F. Baumeister, *Meanings of Life* (Guilford, 1991): 269-93.

[3]Irvin D. Yalom, *Existential Psychotherapy* (Basic Books, 1980); Ernest Becker, "The Spectrum of Loneliness," *Humanitas* 10 (1974): 237-46.

[4]Senada Hajdarevic et al., "You Never Know When Your Last Day Will Come and Your Trip Will Be Over—Existential Expressions From a Melanoma Diagnosis," *European Journal of Oncology Nursing* 18 (2014): 355–61, http://dx.doi.org/10.1016/j.ejon.2014.03.015.

[5]M. Elizabeth Lewis Hall et al., "The Varieties of Redemptive Experiences: A Qualitative Study of Meaning-Making in Evangelical Christian Cancer Patients," *Psychology of Religion and Spirituality* 12, no. 1 (2020): 13-25.

[6]Jeff Greenberg et al., "The Causes and Consequences of a Need for Self-Esteem: A Terror Management Theory," in *Public Self and Private Self*, ed. Roy F. Baumeister (Springer-Verlag, 1986).

[7]Sheldon Solomon et al., *The Worm at the Core: On the Role of Death in Life* (Random House, 2015). Tom Pyszczynski et al., *In the Wake of 9/11: The Psychology of Terror* (American Psychological Association, 2003). Jeff Greenberg et al., "Evidence for Terror Management Theory II: The Effects of Mortality Salience on Reactions to Those Who Threaten or Bolster the Cultural Worldview," *Journal of Personality and Social Psychology* 58, no. 2 (1990): 308-18. Holly A. McGregor et al., "Terror Management and Aggression: Evidence That Mortality Salience Motivates Aggression Against Worldview-Threatening Others," *Journal of Personality and Social Psychology* 74, no. 3 (1998); 590-605.

[8]John R. W. Stott, *The Cross of Christ* (InterVarsity Press, 1986), 160.

[9]Benedict, *The Rule of Saint Benedict* (SPCK, 1931), 6.

[10]Charles Spurgeon, "What Is Your Life?" Sermon 1773, March 30, 1884.

[11]Todd Billings, *The End of the Christian Life* (Brazos, 2020), 116.

[12]Philip J. Cozzolino et al., "Greed, Death, and Values: From Terror Management to 'Transcendence Management' Theory," *Personality and Social Psychology Bulletin* 30 (2004): 278-92.

[13]Karl Barth, *Church Dogmatics*, trans. G. W. Bromiley and Thomas F. Torrance (Hendrickson, 2010), III/4, 591.

[14]Adapted from Theresa Aletheia Noble, *Memento Mori: Prayers on the Last Things* (Pauline Books and Media, 2019).

11. WEAVING OUR STORY OF SUFFERING INTO GOD'S STORY

[1]Jack J. Bauer et al., "Narrative Identity and Eudaimonic Well-Being," *Journal of Happiness Studies* 9 (2008): 81-104.

[2]Dan P. McAdams and Michelle Albaugh, "The Redemptive Self, Generativity, and American Christians at Midlife," in *Autobiography and the Psychological Study of Religious Lives,* ed. Jacob A. Belzen and Antoon Geels (Editions Rodopi, 2008), 255-86.

[3]Dan P. McAdams et al., "Beyond the Redemptive Self: Narratives of Acceptance in Later Life (and in Other Contexts)," *Journal of Research in Personality* 100 (2022): 104286.

[4]Dan P. McAdams et al., "When Bad Things Turn Good and Good Things Turn Bad: Sequences of Redemption and Contamination in Life Narrative and Their Relation to Psychosocial Adaptation in Midlife Adults and in Students," *Personality and Social Psychology Bulletin* 27, no. 4 (2001): 474-85.

[5]Dan P. McAdams, *The Redemptive Self: Stories Americans Live By* (Oxford University Press, 2013).

[6]Karl Barth, "The Strange New World Within the Bible," in *The Word of God and the Word of Man*, trans. Douglas Horton (Peter Smith, 1978), 28-50.

[7]Barth, "Strange New World," 49.

[8]See, for example, Isa. 25:8; 35:10; 60:20; 65: 18-19; Jer. 31:13; cf., Rev. 7:17; 21:4

[9]For a more filled-out approach, see N. T. Wright's description of the five-act play: I. Creation, II. Fall, III. Israel, IV. Jesus, V. Kingdom. The last act is unfinished, but we have the opening scenes (the Gospels) and indications of how the story is meant to end (Revelation). N. T. Wright, *The New Testament and the People of God, Christian Origins and the Question of God*, vol. 1 (Fortress Press, 1992), 141-43.

[10]Oscar Cullman, *Christ and Time* (SCM, 1951).

[11]Cullman, *Christ and Time,* 84.

[12]Cornelius Plantinga Jr., *Not the Way It's Supposed to Be: A Breviary of Sin* (Eerdmans, 1996).

[13]J. D. Plüss, "Testimony," in *A Global Dictionary of Theology: A Resource for the Worldwide Church*, ed. William A. Dyrness and Veli-Matti Kärkkäinen (IVP Academic, 2008): 879.

[14]M. Elizabeth Lewis Hall et al., "Testimony and Meaning: A Qualitative Study of Black Women with Cancer Diagnoses," *Cultural Diversity and Ethnic Minority Psychology* 27, no. 4 (2021): 731.

[15]Timothy Keller, *Walking with God Through Pain and Suffering* (Dutton, 2013), 30.